Kaya Genç is a novelist and essayist from Istanbul whose writing has appeared in the *Paris Review*, the *Guardian*, the *Financial Times*, the *London Review of Books*, *Salon*, *Guernica* magazine, *Sight & Sound*, *The Millions*, the *White Review* and *TIME* magazine, among others. His first novel, *L'Avventura*, was published in 2008. Kaya has a PhD in English literature and is the Istanbul correspondent of *The Believer* and the *LA Review of Books* as well as a contributing editor at *Index on Censorship*. His article for the *LA Review of Books*, 'Surviving the Black Sea', was selected as one of the best non-fiction pieces of 2014 by *The Atlantic*.

'Kaya Genç, a wonderful writer and tireless champion of literature, has done us all a great service by bringing together so many young voices on the Gezi movement. What a marvellous resource for everyone who is interested in this (let's face it) incredibly interesting moment in Turkish history.'

Elif Batuman, *New Yorker* staff writer

'Kaya Genç is one of the most interesting Turkish writers to have emerged in recent years. In his essays as well as his fiction, he converses across borders, while forging his own distinct voice and perspective and challenging dominant narratives.'

Maureen Freely, President of English PEN, author of *The Enlightenment* and translator of Orhan Pamuk

'Kaya Genç's writing is as evocative as it is charming.'

Elif Shafak, bestselling author of *The Architect's Apprentice* and *Honour*

# UNDER THE SHADOW

## Rage and Revolution in Modern Turkey

Kaya Genç

I.B. TAURIS
LONDON · NEW YORK

Published in 2016 by
I.B.Tauris & Co. Ltd
London • New York
www.ibtauris.com

Copyright © 2016 Kaya Genç

The right of Kaya Genç to be identified as the author of this work has been
asserted by the author in accordance with the Copyright, Designs and
Patents Act 1988.

All rights reserved. Except for brief quotations in a review, this book, or
any part thereof, may not be reproduced, stored in or introduced into a
retrieval system, or transmitted, in any form or by any means, electronic,
mechanical, photocopying, recording or otherwise, without the prior
written permission of the publisher.

References to websites were correct at the time of writing.

ISBN: 978 1 78453 457 8
eISBN: 978 1 78672 069 6
ePDF: 978 1 78673 069 5

A full CIP record for this book is available from the British Library
A full CIP record is available from the Library of Congress

Library of Congress Catalog Card Number: available

Cover image: Protestors clash with Turkish riot policemen on the way
to Taksim Square in Istanbul on 3 June 2013, as part of ongoing protests
against the destruction of Gezi Park for a development project. (Bulent
Kilic/AFP/Getty Images)

Cover design: Sandra Friesen

Typeset by Fakenham Prepress Solutions, Fakenham, Norfolk NR21 8NN
Printed and bound by TJ International Ltd, Padstow, Cornwall

MIX
Paper from
responsible sources
FSC® C013056

# Contents

'Who has never been burned in the sun
won't know the value of shadow'
Turkish Proverb

# Preface

Istanbul was once ruled by *keyif*, an old word which means both pleasure and a state of carelessness and joy – especially during springtime. For a long time, I thought it was inevitable that books on Turkey would be full of scenes of Istanbul locals drinking cups of strong Turkish coffee in small seaside restaurants, or others smoking water pipes in cafes perched on hills overlooking the city's Bosphorus Strait – a reminder of an enlightened empire that ruled continents. In April every year, the city's Judas trees blossom and lines of yellow tulips accompany the roads that lead to the city's financial centre, distracting even the most determined money-seekers: an hour to reflect on life can always be found in Istanbul. I have long felt the existence of a silent agreement among Istanbul's locals that they would do anything necessary to keep this state of *keyif* intact. Most people I know in this town, I thought, would never be exposed to protestors clashing with each other on the streets as the sound of gunfire echoes down Istiklal, or the flash of Molotov cocktails and the unbearable smell that lingers when riot police spray pepper gas into crowds, or the terror of tanks on city boulevards.

How brilliantly deceiving appearances can turn out to be. In the last three years, roughly from spring 2013 to autumn 2016, this ancient, Byzantine, laid-back vision of Istanbul has undergone such a startling transformation as to be almost unrecognizable. Nowadays Istanbul's reputation is increasingly that of a target of international terror. Stuck between

Islamic State in Syria, Kurdish-populated cities in northern Iraq, and the eastern borders of the European Union, Turkey has become a dangerous place to live peacefully. It is like a passage between two rooms, or a tunnel between two different cultures, or a massive figure who stretches his arms between two worlds: the European Union which it had long struggled to join, and the troubled, war-torn cities of the Middle East which it had ruled during the reign of the Ottoman Empire.

It is sad to see my country, once best known for its sugary desserts, its magnificent rugs and the glory of its Islamic culture, becoming the site of bombs, political assassinations and street terror. How things change: as late as 2013, it felt like the only possible cause of street violence in Turkey would be the fight between student protestors. Suicide attacks? Car bombs? Tanks on the streets, and soldiers firing at citizens on the Bosphorus bridge? Unthinkable. I remember a subway commute to Istanbul's Taksim Square one day in 2013 when I heard the announcement of an emergency lock-down in the station. I ran to the subway exit and was lucky enough to escape above ground at the last possible moment, as riot police moved in. This was during the Gezi Park events in 2013, a time when the only thing that seemed to threaten the country's peace was the prospect of a demonstration and its suppression.

Nowadays such protests have all but melted into the background. They are replaced by a new, darker, more ominous form of politics: the placing of bombs inside rubbish bins and news about foreign fighters wearing suicide belts walking into tourist groups to kill Europeans. The kidnapping of generals and the killing of anti-coup activists on the streets. What makes this even more depressing is that this was supposed to be a country that had achieved a liberal consensus through a process of 'demilitarization and normalization', and the sidelining of hardliners to make way for moderates and common sense. Only three years have passed since Turkey was described in such a way, and the country has since become such a violent stage for political conflict that its elderly citizens point to the dark period of 1970s radicalism as a worrying example that parallels the present. Istanbul is recovering from a military coup which killed hundreds of civilians. On 28 June 2016, three Islamic State suicide bombers killed 45 people in the lobby of Atatürk Airport.

For some of the people in this book, this moment in Turkey is a moment of release: the release of desires repressed for so long for different reasons. The more philosophically minded would say this is the moment of truth: the replacement of liberal illusions with the cold reality of haves and have-nots, liberals and conservatives, the old versus the young. In the years leading up to the 2013 Gezi protests, all people could speak about in Turkey was reconciliation, consensus and harmony: all signs of order posited against the dastardly prospect of a chaotic era whose arrival needed to be stopped by all means necessary. But dreams of an ordered society were in conflict with the passionate, the hot-headed and the energetic – Turkey's young people. Many on the left and the nationalist right, as well as in the radical Kurdish movement, objected to the early 2010s atmosphere in Turkey that had been forged around the concept of peace and liberalism, warning the country against an all-powerful Turkish state under Recep Tayyip Erdoğan. All the talk about *keyif* and the flourishing tourism on Turkey's Mediterranean coasts, the wisdom of Constantinople's history, the mysterious bazaars of Istanbul now open to the world's tourists: that meant nothing to the young, the radical and the 'othered'. While well-intentioned travellers to Istanbul enjoyed the peace that ruled Turkey, others prepared for war. The disillusioned and the dispossessed were looking for a day of uprisings. Be careful what you wish for, the popular saying goes, because you may end up getting it.

# INTRODUCTION

# Speaking Out

*'This is your future ... if your generation does not fight for it, it will be a disastrous one.'*

Recently I took a walk down Istanbul's central Istiklal Street. Every day here crowds of pedestrians float around in small groups, surrounded by the cries of street vendors and the ding-dongs of *tramvay*, Istiklal's beloved old wooden streetcar that travels up and down this populous shopping quarter from seven in the morning to ten-thirty at night. When I feel overwhelmed by this crowded city I wander by the Bosphorus Strait and watch the reflections of the sun on the slow waves of the Marmara Sea. But on lonelier days I prefer to mix with the crowds of Istiklal and come across new fashions, new people, new ideas. On that Friday I came all the way to the middle of Istiklal, to a square called Galatasaray, to sit down and enjoy a cup of strong black Turkish coffee. A little bell rang as I opened the door to a small and serene coffee shop. Taking a seat, I began listening to a song by the Kurdish singer Aynur Doğan on my headphones, and typed up the opening paragraph of a new chapter in my novel. I felt lucky to be living in such a beautiful and vibrant and history-filled city. As I wrote, I entered my fictional world and felt at peace.

At some point I looked up as the hand of a young man appeared silently against the thick glass of the coffee shop window. The hand banged the glass loudly, passionately, one, two, three times and I saw that he had company: a dark-haired youth carrying a bright flag that bore the colours red, yellow and green, which signalled Turkey's Kurdish political movement. Seconds later, a group of high school students followed behind them and the crowd began to force its way into the shop, signs of panic discernible on their faces. A cup fell and broke. Almost immediately a cloud of smoke enveloped the first activist as the street leading to the square filled grimly with the outlines of heavily armed riot cops marching towards us in single file, chasing this small group of rebels. The barista instantly rushed to the doorway; in an attempt to save her customers from the swiftly approaching cloud of smoke and tear gas, she let the protestors inside, closed and locked the door, and took down the shutters.

For a few moments, in the darkness, it seemed as if we were safe from harm – but that was before we realized the air conditioning was still working. It took 15 seconds for the interior of the five-square-metre room to fill with tear gas. If you have ever come into contact with tear gas you will know how every breath you take burns your insides, how your eyes sting – and my mind, filled with joy, ecstasy and serenity only three minutes ago, was now occupied by the question of whether I would survive this experience. Apparently, while I was travelling through my fictional world, a protest had kicked off in the adjacent square, which the police had forcefully suppressed.

It is a sign of where Turkey is today that nobody was really surprised. Young people are furious in Turkey. So far, the massive protests in Istanbul's Gezi Park in 2013, two years ago on that day, had been the most visible demonstration of this temperament. During a humid, anxious and violent month in Istanbul, it had seemed as if angry Turkish men and women were willing to sacrifice everything in order to change their country. Marching in solidarity in about 90 different locations, young people in Turkey attempted to stage a revolution and were ready to defend their right to protest even against thousands of heavily armed police officers. In epic scenes coloured by the sight of huge water cannons spraying water into crowds of protestors, the days between 28 May and 15 June 2013 shook Turkey and, as I'll show here, changed its political scene beyond return. They brought Turkey's troubled and energetic political, cultural and artistic spheres right to the centre of the international stage. Events that defined the three years since Gezi – from the crisis in Syria to the rise of Islamic State and to the changing relationships with the US and PKK (Kurdistan Workers' Party) – were somewhat energized by the big boom effect Gezi has had on Turkey.

But the roots of this explosion of energy lay deeper, in the country Turkey was before it became 'modern'.

## The Sad Story of Post-Coup Turkey

At the beginning of the 1980s, General Kenan Evren's military dictatorship banned all 'political activities' and imposed almost complete control over all facets of public life. One of the justifications for the coup led by Evren was an Islamist rally organized in the Anatolian city of Konya. In the city where the poet and founder of Sufism, Jalāl ad-Dīn Muhammad Rūmī, breathed his last, thousands of furious protestors shouted slogans protesting Israel's declaration that Jerusalem would be their state's eternal capital. The Konya rally, where crowds reportedly refused to sing the Turkish national anthem, was another expression of a nation which the state apparatus increasingly considered ungovernable. Any political struggle was decisively settled by generals on 12 September 1980, when activists of all political persuasions were imprisoned and the armed forces brought Turkish society back to its Atatürkian factory settings. Generals took the further precaution of locking activists, many of them in their early twenties and with polar opposite political views, in the same cells – the sarcastic message was that prison cells were the proper places for Turkey's youths to resolve their issues.

Once different political views were silenced, the armed forces started patrolling social life. Their first move was to capture the state broadcaster, TRT, from where Kenan Evren announced the start of his military dictatorship. My generation grew up watching TRT, which had a monopoly on broadcasting until 1990 and which put on an endless show of official ceremonies. Programmes advocating different facets of Turkey's official state ideology were the only things to watch, and in particular one endlessly repeated montage of soldiers raising the flag in the morning with a romantic, dreamy view of Mustafa Kemal Atatürk's mausoleum Anıtkabir in the background.

The main message sent to Turkey's citizens was 'go home and leave the streets to us'. The representations of what we today see as Turkish things – from eating *çiğ köfte* to listening to oriental music – were forcefully removed from the public sphere, replaced by an imaginary vision of purity in which the nation had no unruly cultural stains on its surface.

4

Turkey was presented as an indivisible country, an indivisible ideology, an indivisible nation. The role of its citizens was to show total submission to it. As children we watched generals while they pontificated about Turkey's enemies, be they Greece or Syria, and listened as they described the real enemies that existed within: the traitors and 'unlawful elements'. These were described in terms borrowed from the dismal language of genocide: images of bugs, flies and other black-coloured insects.

During this time, the function of the Turkish school system was similar to that of the TV – to teach us the sanctity of the Turkish flag, the national anthem, the school oath. At school we often marched in single file; every gym class for boys was a preparation for our future life in the army. Every school week began with the morning school oath, where pupils from very different cultural and ethnic backgrounds were forced to say they sacrificed their lives 'to the existence of the Turk!' In history classes, we learned about how Turkey had always been mistreated and wronged by its enemies, and how its unity was constantly under threat from evil forces. The 'internal' enemies of the nation were a populous bunch: Islamists, Kurds, feminists, leftists, anarchists, defenders of shari'a, homosexuals. Happily, the armed forces crushed them on our behalf every day. The public sphere was perilous, filled with dangerous Others: gypsies were thieves, Kurds were terrorists, headscarved women were traitors, in every burqa hid a shari'a-supporter, gays were ideological instruments of the corrupt and capitalist West. We were advised to be hardworking, pure and modern citizens, devote our lives to our families, spend time in our homes with people we trusted. Taxis were safer than buses; public places were to be avoided at all times, if possible.

The army's limitless control of all aspects of Turkey's social life continued well into the 1990s, when the military apparatus directed all its energies to destroying dissident political voices, the most prominent of which was the Kurdish movement. The army took its power from the rejected rights of Turkey's Kurds (even the use of the word Kurd was banned before the 2000s when Kurds did not exist in the eyes of the official ideology: they were 'mountain Turks', our sadly less developed fellow countrymen) as well as the systematic torture of their activists, most notoriously in the city of Diyarbakır, whose infamous prison (known as 'the hell of Diyarbakir') saw the deaths by torture or suicide of 34 prisoners during the first years of the military dictatorship. Later, the military dictatorship in eastern Turkey would lead to some of the worst crimes, such as force-feeding Kurdish villagers with faeces, and the Vietnam-style burning of their villages. The complete repression of their rights led the Kurdish movement to go underground in Turkey, while in European countries where many of its militants emigrated, they made criticism of the dictatorship in Turkey public. European countries, especially those which housed first-generation guest workers, witnessed the birth of Islamist or conservative political organizations whose activities were anxiously watched by generals in Ankara. But it was the unacknowledged civil war with Kurdish militants that really terrified the generals – this fear caused the deaths of more than thirty thousand citizens, the burnings and forced cleansing of villages, and a complete suppression of all media reporting on what was actually taking place in the country. The so-called Kurdish question destroyed Kenan Evren and his fellow generals' efforts to present Turkey as a peaceful country to the world, and made its black mark on the 1990s. The PKK's (Kurdistan Workers'

Party) response to the generals was equally brutal and bloody, claiming the lives of numberless innocents, following attacks in towns and cities.

This mixture of officialdom, statism and the violent denial of any form of dissent proved pervasive. As the armed forces continued to mould society in its own image and its rivals went underground and became radicalized, Turkey became a buttoned-up nation, a space where any form of challenge to discipline was punished, not only in the infamous State Security Courts (DGM) that purportedly protected the unity of the state, but also in schools, barracks, offices and newspaper columns. Teachers would slap pupils in the face who did not sing the national anthem; wearing clothes with the 'dangerous colours' (red, yellow and green) of the Kurdish movement could land you in a police station. This era of dictatorship in Turkey, where total submission to the state apparatus was advocated seven days a week, 24 hours a day in school and on television, was a triumph of the state's ideological instruments. When dissident voices were invited onto television programmes, young patriots in the audience would proudly destroy their arguments; I remember one programme where fresh-faced 18-year-olds sang a nationalist marching song so loudly that the dissidents on the show who questioned the official ideology could no longer be heard, to the joy of the presenter.

## The Tall Man and the Shadow

Fifteen years ago, in 2002, its first-ever general election, a newly formed political party won a shockingly huge victory in Turkey. It seemed to offer a new hope – a blend of capitalism, conservatism, integration with the EU and strong partnership with the US. It was a revelation to those who, like me, had lived through the military coups and oppressive propaganda of the 1980s when the state allowed you to live in Turkey as long as you agreed to conceal your identity and behave in the way expected of you.

Thus begun the decade of the AK Party, superficially headed by the charismatic speaker Abdullah Gül, a Western university graduate and an Islamic Development Bank executive. The real leader of the party, meanwhile, was a man well known in Turkey for his previous career as the successful, if divisive, mayor of Istanbul. Nicknamed 'the tall man', he had been banned from political life and imprisoned in the city of Kırklareli in 1999 for four months because of a rebellious poem he read at a political rally – Turkey is a place where poetry and language has always been important, as Erdoğan knows personally. 'He can't even become a reeve [head of a neighbourhood]!' announced the mainstream *Hürriyet* daily at the time. The old feared him; the media was scared of him; for his supporters, though, this energetic young man promised a new direction for the country.

Erdoğan's first term in office was greeted by congratulatory op-eds from the *New York Times,* the *Guardian* and the *Economist.* Chris Morris, the BBC's Turkey correspondent at the time, was so impressed by the societal transformation offered by Erdoğan's team that he named his book *The New Turkey: The Quiet Revolution on the Edge of Europe.* Endorsed by a wide range of world leaders, from Tony Blair to Gerhard Schroeder to Daniel Cohn-Bendit, the AK Party's economic policies seemed to be set to release the potential of the country, with Turkey becoming the sixteenth largest economy in the world, its GDP trebling to 820 billion dollars by 2013.

But perhaps the real success of the party for foreign politicians and policy advisors was its fulfilment of the perceived need for a model country for the Muslim world in the aftermath of the September 11 attacks in the US. Democratic, secular and progressive, Turkey then seemed to be at the beginning of a more stable relationship with the Middle East. As with so many things detailed in this book, this was partly an illusion. The following decade has proved how the new government's agenda featured a potential future shift towards Islamic values which would be inspirational for movements like the Muslim Brotherhood in Egypt and other Islamist political parties – not exactly what the US foreign policy experts expected from Turkey's new role but resulting in increasingly better results at general elections for conservatives: a success, in electoral terms.

While the rest of the world fawned, all was not well in Turkey itself, as the AK slowly began to resemble the parties it had once sought to oppose. On 29 September 2001, Turkish novelist and future Nobel laureate Orhan Pamuk published a think piece in the *Guardian*, in which he warned the world against the repercussions of a severe punishment of 'Islamists' through military force. 'The wealthy, pro-modernist class who founded the Turkish republic reacted to resistance from the poor and backward sectors of society not by attempting to understand them, but by law-enforcement measures, interdictions, and the army', Pamuk wrote, in a reference to the 1980 coups. 'In the end, the modernization effort remained half-finished, and Turkey became a limited democracy in which intolerance prevailed. Now, as cries for an east–west war echo throughout the world, I am afraid of the world turning into a place like Turkey, governed almost permanently by martial law.'

When Recep Tayyip Erdoğan took the reins of power, not everyone was sure whether he was the man to represent a nation whose transformation from an empire to a nation state in the 1920s was built strictly on the republican principle of the separation of religion and state. Erdoğan repeatedly argued that the fundamental idea could not work in Turkey, since it ran counter to the realities of a devout Turkish society. Before Erdoğan there were public clashes between the state and headscarved Turkish girls; veiled women were physically prevented from entering universities and working in the public sector. These policies had alienated hundreds of thousands of conservative voters. It was his pledge to change this, alongside imposing an economic model to create a prosperous middle class, that won Erdoğan's party the election.

In a now infamous conversation with a journalist in 2008, the prime minister had asked rhetorically: 'What if the headscarf is a symbol? Even if it were a political symbol, does that give one the right to ban it?' As a challenge to Turkey's constitution, this was as direct as anyone had been for many decades. It led to a massive crisis at the upper echelons of the state. Turkey's chief prosecutor Abdurrahman Yalçınkaya filed a formal request to the Constitutional Court to immediately close down the AK Party. As late as 2008, the government had still not been able to lift the ban on headscarves at state universities. Yalçınkaya's charge of violating the separation of religion and state was rejected by only one vote and the AK Party closely escaped closure.

By the mid-2000s the AK Party's vote base had greatly expanded since its first election. But the support, at least in Istanbul, was a silent one: a muted approval of the country's 'normalization', its integration with foreign markets and the expansion in its creative industries. This was the age of bankers, finance, communication, internet and advertisement: for many, employment in one of the global multinationals was the best thing that could happen in life, while their political-activist parents, who had lived through the worst of the 1980s, accused them of the crime of being apolitical.

As the economy continued to soar, many – even on the right – were not happy with the political world Erdoğan was fostering. In 2007, hundreds of thousands of citizens marched in Ankara and Istanbul, two weeks before the parliamentary vote on the selection of the new Turkish president. The organizers of those 'Republican Marches' asked protestors to 'safeguard the republic' and strongly opposed the election of Erdoğan to the highest seat in the state, which they accused him of undermining. The majority of those protestors will have attended the Gezi uprising in 2013, constituting its so-called 'republican' and 'nationalist' bases. The BBC titled its report about the marches 'Secular rally targets Turkish PM', describing how 'the area was packed with people, many of them draped in the red-and-white national flag and chanting anti-Islamic slogans. "Turkey is secular and will remain secular forever", they shouted.'

Many of these were not left-wing rabble-rousers, Erdoğan's natural opposition in the eyes of many Western observers, but hardcore nationalists. One of the organizers of the event was Atatürkçü Düşünce Derneği (Atatürkist Thought Organization). Its leader voiced the frustration of protestors in the following way: 'We are living in times where it is a crime to say "How happy is the one who says I am a Turk", but then if you say "How happy is the one who says I am a Kurd or an Armenian" then this is packaged as human rights or

11

democracy ... As a Turkish citizen, as a nationalist, I send my gratitude to Turkish armed forces. I call all of those who are proud to say "How happy is the one who says I am a Turk" to public squares ...' The slogan of the protest march was 'Neither the US nor the EU, what we want is a completely independent Turkey!'

In other words, Turkey's society was divided into two groups in the last years of the noughties. On the one side stood the AK Party, now with the support of nearly 50 per cent of the electorate, as well as the rhetorical services of conservative and left-liberal opinion leaders. On the other side stood socialists, communists, nationalists and republicans who, despite their differences, were united in their opposition to what they considered to be the party's attempt to undermine the foundations of the secular nation state. Six years after the AK Party came to power, this tension would erupt as a result of a court case that would change everything in Turkish politics.

## Books are Bombs: The Trial

In 2008, Turkey had just one journalist in prison. By December 2012 Reporters Without Borders stated that, 'with a total of 72 media personnel currently detained, of whom at least 42 journalists and four media assistants are being held in connection with their media work, Turkey is now the world's biggest prison for journalists'. The Committee to Protect Journalists' 2007 report described this state of affairs in the following way: 'Over the last decade, Turkey made noticeable progress in improving its press freedom record. Among the world's leading jailers of journalists in the 1990s, Turkey has nearly ended the practice of putting reporters behind bars; at year's end, there was one reporter in prison for his work. Much of the improvement was the result of comprehensive legal reforms undertaken by the government in recent years.'

In the years preceding 2008, there was a relaxation of laws that in the past had criminalized writers who wrote about issues once perceived as taboo. It had now briefly become easier, for example, to write and talk about issues such as the mass killings of Armenians in 1915 or the suppressed rights and the inhumane treatment of Kurds by the state. Those two issues had been central to the conviction of dissident voices during the 1980s and 1990s. For a country in whose history words and writers have played such a central role, despite the continuous attempts of a state apparatus that never ceases to put pressure on them, merely talking about such issues was as significant as solving them. The demand of Turkey's people was to lift the state's ideological monopoly on historical issues that so strongly defined the present time. Only then would they be transferred to the hands of writers and academics where they could be judiciously analysed. Turkey's transformation, in four years, from a country that seemed to have partly fixed its freedom of expression problem into one of the leading jailers of journalists in the world was the result of a court case which began on 28 July 2008. On that day an Istanbul court accepted a 2,455-page indictment only a few in the media managed to read, but whose central claim everyone learned in the following days.

The state persecutor claimed that a shadowy nationalist organization had been caught in the act of plotting a bloody military coup against the country. Eighty-six defendants were accused of being members of this alleged organization, named Ergenekon (located in the valleys of the Altay Mountains,

Ergenekon has long been mythologized by Turkish nationalists as the place from where Turks first emerged), and its alleged members included İlhan Selçuk and Doğu Perinçek, two prominent names of the left-nationalist Turkish opposition. The former, the editor-in-chief of *Cumhuriyet* newspaper, was a student leader in his youth, a famous member of the Turkish left and the author of numerous books. The latter, a theoretician and leader of the Workers' Party, had led an influential political movement whose youth branch, Öncü Gençlik (Pioneer Youth) was particularly active in universities.

From the day the first police operations began, the Ergenekon case dominated Turkey's news agenda. With fresh arrests every few months, it helped form an impression that the Turkish state was intent on imprisoning all those who opposed its policies, since the actions of all the leading names of the left-nationalist movement were meticulously tracked and investigated before they were arrested in so-called 'dawn operations' – dragged out of their houses and into police cars in front of flashing television cameras. When prominent figures in journalism and academia, names like Yalçın Küçük and Soner Yalçın, found themselves behind bars, it became clear what was happening, although it was little known outside Turkey's borders since foreign media didn't really report it.

At the time, the argument of the government and its supporters in the media was that had it not been for those arrests, a military coup would have taken place, bringing Turkey back to the morning of 12 September 1980. Some of the accused had been ardent ultra-nationalists, asking for the punishment of liberal-minded novelists and journalists under the infamous Article 301 of the Turkish penal code that made it a criminal offence to 'offend Turkishness', which many state prosecutors interpreted as the official narrative of

Turkish nationalism. Since suspects in the Ergenekon trials included dozens of military personnel, all of them accused of attempting to stage a coup against the elected government, many thought the Ergenekon trial was the lesser of two evils – it seemed to protect them from the wrath of nationalists, who would lock them up if given the chance. For those who attended the Republican Marches and saw the government as an underminer of the secular republic, on the other hand, it was the military that was the lesser of two evils – it seemed to protect them from the wrath of Islamists.

The year 2008 saw the completion of Silivri Penitentiaries Campus, the biggest penal facility not just in Turkey but in the whole of Europe. Most Ergenekon suspects were sent to Silivri, where they awaited trial for months and, in some cases, years. Some died while awaiting their trials.

The number of those held inside Silivri since 20 October 2008 greatly increased the following year, when the courtroom inside the campus was no longer able to hold all suspects. As the list of convicts in the court case increased, the sense of frustration grew in the country. In the eyes of left-liberal and conservative newspapers Turkey was cleansing itself of its nationalist stains; for nationalists and socialists, in contrast, these were sham trials used to silence Turkey's youth. 'This is your future', a relative told me after watching together news footage of new arrests on TV. 'If your generation does not fight for it, it will be a disastrous one.'

Even when the names of Ahmet Şık and Nedim Şener, two internationally renowned investigative journalists who had devoted their careers to unearthing relationships inside the state, were added to the list of suspects, many left-liberal voices continued to be silent, while international news organizations' interest in the trials remained minimal. Television channels aired videos of their arrests; Şık's final words before being placed inside the police car ('Those who touch it are burned') were particularly moving, leading to speculation and debate in the following weeks. This was becoming part of a pattern: from Mustafa Balbay, the Ankara bureau chief of *Cumhuriyet*, to writer Erol Mütercimler, imprisonment of journalists and activists had turned into a daily occurrence. Other names, like Adnan Türkkan, the founder of the youth association Türkiye Gençlik Birliği (Union of Youth) were added to the list of detained, and news of fresh arrests kept on coming every morning. The arrested activists and journalists were often taken from their beds, in front of their families. Locked up in Silivri, they were prevented from seeing their children grow up. Those events produced a sense of panic, helplessness and anger.

With every fresh move in the trials, newspapers ran angry headlines, accusing the government of building a fascist state where all forms of opposition were stifled. The majority of the arrested accused Hizmet (Service), a business interest group, of being behind the events, arguing that the common point of all the arrestees was their opposition to, or the investigation of, Hizmet's activities. Headed by Fethullah Gülen, a retired cleric living in Pennsylvania, the Hizmet movement was seen as an influential business group made up of young, devoted followers, many of whom were just starting in life, as well as wealthy business people running the country's biggest circulation newspaper and the largest bank. According to imprisoned journalist Şık, who was working on a book named *The Imam's Army*, followers of Gülen were effectively running Turkey's police department and potentially responsible for covering up the murder of Hrant Dink, the assassinated editor of the Armenian-Turkish weekly *Agos*.

In a comment he made at the Parliamentary Assembly of the Council of Europe, while being questioned about *The Imam's Army* which, even before it was published, led to its author's imprisonment, Erdoğan defended this blatant attack on the freedom of expression. 'I did not personally make the decision about this book which, people say, has not yet been published', he said. 'It is a crime to use a bomb; it is a crime, also, to use parts that make up a bomb. If someone informs the police about the possibility of a bomb going off, shouldn't security forces go and take those parts away?' The bomb parts in Erdoğan's metaphor corresponded to portions of text which would later be brought together and published under the title *000 Kitap,* a reference to the file name Şık gave to his yet unpublished book while it was still a Word document on his computer's desktop.

Shortly after, in an interview with the television channel NTV, Erdoğan defended the arrests of investigative journalists. 'There are some books that are more effective than bombs', he said, before smiling self-confidently. For many his answer came as a shock – Erdoğan himself had been imprisoned in 1999 because of a poem he read at a public rally (incidentally, the poem was penned by Ziya Gökalp, the Turkish nationalist poet and sociologist best known for his 'Ergenekon'-themed verses). It was now made painfully clear what the reward of investigative journalists writing about secret groups in the state apparatus or corruption in the police department would be: decades-long prison sentences in Silivri.

It was around this time that people started calling Erdoğan 'the Sultan': a protective figure for one half of Turkey's society, an oppressive one for the other.

## Turkey and Dissent

Imagine yourself as a young citizen of Turkey in the first months of 2013. You are part of a country that has a 16.6 per cent young population, making it the youngest in Europe. You live in a country where cultures of entrepreneurship and dissent are equally rich, while a struggle in the public sphere, seemingly never-ending, energizes the country every morning. Wearisome though it may frequently appear, the dissent in Turkish society provides an endless reserve of energy for young people like you. The discourse of perfect democracy and claims of Turkey being a 'model country' for the Islamic world, you feel, are merely the surface of things: behind the glossy facade lies a reality not recognized by either the commentariat or politicians, a reality only you can see. You feel as if you are the one who should act, before it is too late.

Every student in Turkey who graduated from the country's nationalist education system is inescapably familiar with Mustafa Kemal Atatürk's address to the youth, hung on the walls of all classrooms in the country. It is a call to action to youth in the face of potential danger:

Oh Turkish Youth!

Your first duty is to preserve and defend forever Turkish independence and the Turkish Republic.

This is the only foundation of your existence and of your future. This foundation is your most precious treasure.

In the future, too, there will be malevolent people at home and abroad who will wish to deprive you of this treasure. If one day you have to defend your independence and your Republic, you will not tarry to weigh the circumstances before taking up your duty. These possibilities and circumstances may be extremely unfavourable. The enemies nursing designs against your independence and your republic, may have behind them a victory unprecedented in the annals of the world. It may come to pass that, by violence and ruse, all the fortresses of your beloved fatherland will be occupied, all its shipyards captured, all its armies dispersed, and every part of the country invaded. And what is sadder and graver than all these circumstances is that the people in power inside the country may be blind, misguided. They may even be traitors. The men in power may join their personal interest to the political designs of the invaders. The country may be impoverished, ruined and exhausted.

Oh, Child of Turkey's future, even in these circumstances it is your duty to save Turkey's independence and the Turkish Republic.

You will find the power you need in the noble blood in your veins.

As a young citizen of the republic you find it easy to identify with this 'child of Turkey's future', 'the Turkish youth', this mysterious 'you' whose only foundation for her existence is to 'preserve and defend forever Turkish independence and the Turkish Republic'. For secularist youth, it is they who should now take action against the oppressors of their country; for conservative youth, meanwhile, it is they who should defend the country against those who undermine its stability.

The historical echoes of the address to the youth are impossible to ignore. It is equally important to remember that Mustafa Kemal Atatürk's address has been heard, read and interpreted by everybody in the country. This is one of the reasons why in *Under the Shadow* I will show that the way to understand angry young Turkey is not to look at one group of activists, but to look at a much wider range that includes both the political movement represented by the current government and those that show the most powerful resistance to it. I will show how it is not only 'young seculars' or 'young leftists' or 'young liberals' who are politicized in today's Turkey; 'conservatives' who voted for the current government have similarly been defined by their frustration and discontent, which they have successfully transformed into a political organization. They see themselves as gravediggers of the country's Westernization-obsessed classes, much in the same way the angry young men and women in Gezi Park see themselves as gravediggers of the country's 'normalization' through capitalism.

The protests in 2013 were, in that sense, part of a revolution – one that failed to change the balance of power (it even made the AK Party stronger, as I will explain later) while showing the vitality of freedom of expression. The events activated the political energies of the entirety of civil society. The uprising of Turkey's youth came close to destroying Turkish democracy; had protestors taken control of the prime minister's office, it could have inflicted a blow to a democratic system based on popular elections. Surprisingly, however, the uprising ended up enlivening Turkey's democracy, throwing a handful of cold water in the face of its citizens.

Turkey, in its anger and youth, had spoken. Around eight thousand people were injured during the protests, hundreds of them seriously. In terms of the intensity of its rage, it far surpassed Occupy events in London and New York. Eleven people died during the uprising. In the following months in

Istanbul there was a new march, a new Occupy movement every week. Meanwhile the government changed its mind about the country's enemies, accepted that Ergenekon was a sham trial, and started arresting members of the Hizmet movement with the assistance of previously imprisoned and now released people once accused of plotting to overthrow the government.

How did we get here? Why did young people, many of them highly educated and with an awful lot to lose, make the decision to wear masks, clash with the police and occupy a public park which they defended with their lives? Why have more than three million citizens in Turkey protested, and risked their careers and safety, so as to be able to head out and yell their anger? How have the opposing sides in Turkey's polarized society spent all their time clashing with each other, while the country stands on a precipice, between Syria, Islamic State and a Europe in chaos? How did hope for societal change in 2013 result in violence, instability and annihilation in the years that followed?

# CHAPTER ONE

# Young, Turk and Furious

In Turkey, it is considered uncool to not be a rebel at college. The law-abiding student who follows every rule is called an *inek* (cow). Girls like rebellious boys; boys fall for rebellious girls. The future prospects of a rebel are seen as more attractive than those of an academic achiever. The classic 'how we met' story of the parents of my generation (and the parents of most of the interviewees for this book) features a rebellious boy and a rebellious girl who meet in the classroom or the canteen of a college. They attend marches together; they look after one another under the oppressive regime of this or that prime minister or general; they get married under interesting and dangerous times, backgrounded by their country's politics, which they recount to their children when old age presses upon them.

Remember: this is the country where the *jeune Turks* phenomenon was born. The term originally referred to a new generation of Ottoman citizens who wanted to reform their country, before 'Young Turk' gained an international meaning. 'A young person eager for radical change to the established order' is the definition offered by the Oxford Dictionary: to be a young Turk means to be ontologically a rebel.

Today, if a Turkish citizen thinks of her ancestors who lived a century ago, it is this image of a *jeune Turk* that materializes in front of her: being a rebel in our youth is in our genes, as it were. All the best minds in Ottoman society and the Turkish republic, at least those in the school books, were rebels.

Although they had diametrically opposing views – from defending shari'a rule to arguing in support of a working-class dictatorship inside Turkey – those figures have been fighting the state and risking prosecution and long prison sentences for defending their views for at least a century. The call of the rebellious spirit is rarely unanswered here: only the dull and the uninspired *do not* rebel in their youth. Such is the conventional wisdom.

When young people rebel here, the elderly and the powerful are expected to listen, which they only very rarely do. The Ottoman Sultan Abdul Hamid II did not listen to the republican youth when it rebelled; the president of single-party rule, Ismet Inonu did not listen to the communist youth when it rebelled. The 60 years of Turkish democracy have seen youth and state in constant struggle, mostly an outcome of this denial of dialogue with the youth.

Not that Turkey's youth is eager to compromise in any political debate: doing so is seen as weak and unacceptable. *Omurgasız* (spineless) is among the worst things you can be called in Turkey; selling out one's youthful ideals, making u-turns, succumbing to any form of compromise are seen as dastardly acts. People with passionate, uncompromising and never-bending wills are preferred over those with more conciliatory, diplomatic and seemingly opportunistic characteristics. The same applies to private relationships (thus the attraction of the rebellious youth) and the political sphere alike: leaders, of both left- and right-wing ideologies, are expected to have perfectly consistent life stories wherein the devotion to their political cause is not once compromised.

Such is the environment into which young people are born in Turkey. No wonder the country's young progressives and conservatives are so stubborn in their defence of their political ideas: anger, rebellion and youth have become synonymous in the historical and political psyche of Turkey. The *jeune Turk* spirit of the 1900s has stood the test of geography and time.

On the night of 27 May 2013, a 21-year-old college freshman was returning to his flat in Istanbul's old Armenian neigh-bourhood Samatya when he received some alarming news. Minutes earlier a demolition machine had attempted to cut down a tree in a public park in Taksim that the freshman, Cenk Yürükoğulları, had spent the past week campaigning to save. Upon seeing the news on his Twitter timeline, Yürükoğulları instinctively checked his watch. It was 11.30 p.m.; the last buses from Samatya to Taksim had already departed. But he could still take a *dolmuş* – one of those large cars, a mixture of a cab and a bus, that only starts when it is filled with passengers. Yürükoğulları, a student of conservation, telephoned a friend, a master's student in the field of archaeology who lived close by in the same neighbourhood, to ask whether he would like to come with him. The answer was positive; their *dolmuş* moved from Samatya at midnight; half an hour later they reached Taksim. Most residents of Istanbul use those vehicles to return home from their night shifts or to go to Taksim for a bit of late-night entertainment. Yürükoğulları and his friend's ride to Taksim was about quite a different matter. Those two angry young men were about to start the biggest protest Turkey had ever witnessed in its modern history.

It was a warm and damp night, heady with the scents of the 606 trees that filled the 98,000-square-metre park lying in front of them, concealed in darkness. As they walked among the black trees, Yürükoğulları and his friend saw shadows moving

27

swiftly from one tree to another. More than two dozen people had congregated near the exit of the park. As they neared those shadows they distinguished shapes of construction workers behind demolition machines, who were arguing with protestors. Now Yürükoğulları was able to identify those shadowy figures: over the course of the previous week he had worked with them near the entrance of the Taksim subway station, distributing handouts which demanded an immediate halt to the construction, inside Gezi Park, of an Ottoman-style barracks that would serve as a shopping mall – a weird and unpopular idea which they were sure would upset the public if only people heard about the project through their protest movement.

Having temporarily stopped the workers, the 30-strong group of protestors started holding a small forum to discuss what to do next. While that happened, Yürükoğulları and his friend pitched two small tents inside the park. They joked about possible parallels between what they were getting ready to do (occupy Gezi Park) and Occupy protests in Wall Street, New York. 'Just imagine our protest snowballing into something like Occupy Taksim!' Yürükoğulları joked. 'How about Occupy Istanbul?' his friend joked back. 'No way,' Yürükoğulları responded, '*that* would never happen.'

After the forum about future strategies, one protestor removed a canvas signboard placed there by municipality workers. When Yürükoğulları got his hands on the object, he couldn't help but smile – the young man had been doing graffiti since his high school years. He disappeared into the darkness, only to return moments later with a can of paint. It was recycle time. Yürükoğulları sprayed the words 'We Are On Duty To Protect Gezi Park' on the canvas. This was the first graffiti of the movement – there would be many more.

That night the young conservation student tried to sleep in his small tent where there was little space and air. He decided to get out and take a walk in the park. The trees and the sky seemed mysterious and beautiful. In a contemplative mood, Yürükoğulları wondered what he was doing in a public park in the wee hours of a weekday. How had he reached this point? A shiver went down his spine as Yürükoğulları remembered the machine-gun-carrying riot cops who had been living in a makeshift police station installed in the park during the past month. He still remembered how they intimidated passers-by (mostly tourists walking to or from their hotels adjacent to Gezi) merely by the look of their riot gear. When he saw some lights in the distance Yürükoğulları feared that they came from the cops ... but no, they were nowhere to be seen. He felt tired; it had been a long day of travelling from one neighbourhood to another; the discussions with activists in the forum continued to echo in his mind. Yürükoğulları started dozing off.

When he woke up at 6 a.m. to the sounds of twittering birds, the young man realized he had visitors. Complete strangers on their way to work had stopped by the tents, leaving pastries and plastic plates filled with warm *poğaça*, the kind of cheese-filled scones Turks love to have for breakfast. Many of those *poğaça*-bringers had heard about the protestors through social media and came to say hello.

'I started that day greatly motivated', Yürükoğulları tells me in a posh cafe called Kitchenette a few hundred metres away from the park. He wears a colourful pullover and together we watch the snow as it falls on the beautiful winter day outside. Gezi Park is, once again, deleted from our view – this time under a blinding whiteness rather than the darkness of that May night. I am mildly surprised to hear that Yürükoğulları had never come to Kitchenette before.

'It is not easy to remember exactly how things happened after all we lived through', he says, his hands around the coffee cup. Because of the chaotic way in which the Gezi events ended, Yürükoğulları finds it difficult to focus his mind on the first hours of the protests.

'It was around noon when we saw around a hundred municipal workers and riot cops walking towards our two tents', he remembers. In minutes Yürükoğulları found himself getting punched in the face by one of them, the shock of which made him collapse on his tent. 'They then took our tents and walked away.'

But removing their two tiny tents helped little in stopping the protests; rather, it had the opposite effect. More people started heading to the park, pitching new tents. Yürükoğulları was no longer alone with a handful of people: he was now one among many.

On his second night there, a delivery man arrived carrying two sandwiches and a plastic bottle of water.

'Cenk Yürükoğulları!' he shouted.

'This must be a misunderstanding', the young man replied. 'I didn't order any sandwiches.'

The delivery man handed him a piece of paper. He said it was a note from the buyer. '*Cenk Bey* [Mister Cenk],' it read, 'I study engineering at Kütahya Dumlupınar University. I am not a rich man and this is the most I could do for you. I just wanted to show I am in solidarity with you. I can't be with you there now but my heart is with you. *Afiyet olsun* [Enjoy your meal]!'

The next day a Domino's delivery man arrived. With 250 boxes of pizza next to him, the guy seemed to be on the first stop of a long list of deliveries.

'Cenk Yürükoğulları!' he shouted.

'This must be a misunderstanding', the young man replied.

'I'm totally broke, man. Not a penny in my pockets. I eat pizza maybe once a month. How can I afford 250 boxes of pizza?'

'The payments are all taken care of', the delivery man said. 'Some people created a special account for protestors who stay at the park. You can have all the 250 boxes for free.'

The rest of the day was spent distributing slices of pizza to protestors.

'Everyone seemed ecstatic', Yürükoğulları remembers, sipping his coffee and looking in the direction of the park. 'It was as if we didn't have a worry in the world.'

Yürükoğulları was born in 1991 in Istanbul. He defines his family as working class – 'but like most working-class families, they thought of themselves as middle class. They are middle class in terms of cultural affiliations and working class in terms of their actual income.' Yürükoğulları's parents sent him to schools in Ortaköy and Levent. They picked those neighbourhoods so that he stayed out of trouble and remained 'clean'.

Despite their attempts at keeping him away from trouble Yürükoğulları found himself attracted to rebellious ideas. In high school he refused to read the national anthem during Monday ceremonies; he was irritated by what he saw as the militarist tone of the school discourse. 'For nationalists and Muslims all is well since they find it easy to express their views', he tells me. 'If you have even the slightest objection to the nationalist discourse, if you are just a tiny bit egalitarian and libertarian ... then you are in trouble.'

Most boys at Yürükoğulları's high school dressed up like figures from the popular television show *Kurtlar Vadisi* (The Valley of the Wolves) in which macho, mafioso figures in black suits kill enemies of the Turkish state, so as to protect it from heinous foes.

Not long after he started high school Yürükoğulları, too, wanted to belong. He became a member of a political group called Devrimci Liseliler (Revolutionary High Schoolers). The group rejected wearing uniforms and opposed the unfairness of the exam system, the homophobic undertones of textbooks and the gradual privatization of the school system. 'It was a network, a protected space against oppression', Yürükoğulları remembers. 'We published magazines, distributed stickers and reached people like us.'

In January 2007, when he was 16, Yürükoğulları came across shocking images on TV. An ultra-nationalist assassin had put a bullet into the head of the editor of the Armenian-Turkish weekly newspaper *Agos* metres away from its offices. Dink had long been under attack from Turkish secular-nationalists who had despised his critique of the treatment of Armenians at the hands of Ottoman Young Turks in the 1910s. On the day Dink was shot from behind, Yürükoğulları decided that enough was enough. He got hundreds of stickers from a civil society group called 'Hrant's Friends' that supported a thorough investigation of Dink's murder. 'What Happened on January 19?' asked the stickers he carried home. When Yürükoğulları started sticking them inside his high school, a group of ten pupils attacked him. His complaints to his supervisors came to nothing. Days after the murder, Yürükoğulları not only had to put up with being beaten, but also had to listen to history classes whose nationalist Turkish narrative – 'We never murdered Armenians. They murdered us' – Dink had critiqued in his writings.

When they learned about his political views, Yürükoğulları's parents were somewhat anxious about their son's activism, but they did not oppose him. 'At the end of the day they knew I was searching for truth', he says. 'In high school they were like, "oh don't do this stuff now, Cenk, you can always do it later at uni". Then when I started college they were like, "oh don't do this stuff now, Cenk, you will do it later when you get married!"'

During those years Yürükoğulları was reading two newspapers: the liberal *Taraf* and the left-wing *Radikal*. He had questions in his mind: was Turkey's main opposition party CHP (the People's Republican Party) a left-wing party or a nationalist one? Soon afterwards CHP and Kemalists organized the so-called Republic Protests; what should he do, attend or stay at home? 'I thought hard about this and came to the conclusion that what people attending those marches demanded was a military coup', Yürükoğulları says. 'Their demands stood against my libertarian stance. So I decided against attending.'

In 2010, having thought long about Turkish nationalism, Yürükoğulları made another decision, this time a more crucial one that would have a lasting influence on his life: he became a conscientious objector. This takes guts in a country where military service is mandatory (around six months for college graduates and 16 months for high school graduates) and where pupils are taught at school, *Her Türk Asker Doğar* ('All Turks are born as soldiers'). 'I just don't feel like part of any state in the world', Yürükoğulları explains. 'I imagined a world without any states ... And I did not want to kill, or die, for anyone. At high school we were raised with the motto "May my existence be a gift to the Turk's existence!" For me, betraying this motto was the most ethical thing to do. That's why I have became a conscientious objector.'

Yürükoğulları found similar-minded people at college. 'We talk to friends who have experience in working life ... they tell us about how people working in offices are unable to talk critically about life', he says, not at all looking forward to a white-collar career in an office. 'It felt better to be part of the student movement in Istanbul University which dates back to Ottoman times. There I find people with similar concerns and thoughts. But I am aware that once I get out of that bell glass, there won't be many people like me outside.' But then he can always find protestors outside, as he did in Gezi Park.

A few years ago, Yürükoğulları developed a habit: he started painting on the carriage walls of public trains. He liked the adrenaline that came with the experience. It was around this time he became active in protests against the gentrification of Istanbul. 'I realized that Turkey has long stopped being a lawful country', he says. 'Before the protests, I attended a concert inside the park to protest its prospective destruction. They have set up this police station at the heart of the city. Their station was kind of a panopticon overlooking the park.

'The crucial development that opened our eyes was the gentrification process in Taksim. It was announced that shopkeepers working in the area would be displaced by employees of a new shopping mall. They wanted to cleanse Taksim of any form of political expression; they wanted to turn Taksim into a touristic place for elites; they wanted to change Taksim forever.' The municipality removed outdoor tables from cafes and reportedly instructed bar owners not to sell beer for less than 10 lira. 'They displaced Kurds, LGBTI people, transsexuals, Arabs and Roma people', Yürükoğulları says. 'Together we were entering the era of concrete. It was all about construction projects for the elite from then on.'

In 2013 May Day protests in Istanbul's Taksim Square were banned by the municipality. Yürükoğulları was appalled by the decision. He watched on TV the cops taking into custody any group that attempted any protest on Istiklal Avenue (Istanbul's Oxford Street), located a stone's throw from the park. The blanket ban on public protests meant that even if five people started walking together on Istiklal and shouted a slogan about, say, animal rights, they would be surrounded by the riot police, who during those months dispersed protestors dozens of times using pepper gas, to the dismay of pedestrians. Tourists were shocked to find themselves subjected to huge amounts of pepper gas on summer days. Yürükoğulları says he met many elderly people who scolded the cops during such events. They said things like: 'Come on, you are our sons after all, why are you so angry at us?' Such episodes gave him hope and courage.

During the Gezi protests, Yürükoğulları spent 15 days in the park, visiting his Balat apartment only twice. He was never alone: apart from fellow protestors, his parents visited him in the park. His younger relatives were in the barricades built around the park to keep away the cops. Meanwhile Yürükoğulları stayed in his little tent and had numerous responsibilities. 'Everything was done voluntarily there', he tells me. 'We had built there a non-hierarchical, non-authoritarian system. It felt like the Paris Commune! The 15 days I had spent there felt like a full year ... It was finals time at school but I decided against leaving the park. I said to myself, "Cenk, the things you have been experiencing here are probably more important for you than a mid-term". I was a freshman after all. "This is not something I can't fix", I thought.'

As the days went by, the young man could see on his Twitter feed how mainstream media started focusing on the particulars of the protestors. They were accused of being foreigners in the pay of foreign governments; they were portrayed as innocent Turkish youth deceived by an ominous mind-control technique named *telekinesis* employed by big shots at power centres in New York and London. 'The media antagonized us. The government agitated the cops. Many among us were scared. I wasn't. I stayed there until the final moment. When the cops attacked the park using hundreds of gas capsules, I was still inside, standing tall next to my tent.'

But that was for one moment. Then it was not possible to stay there any more. So Yürükoğulları started running; he ran approximately a mile; the sounds and explosions and screams were left behind him as he reached Maçka Parkı, a large public park in the adjacent neighbourhood. There he had to wake up from the dream he had been living for the past two weeks. It was a new day.

Gezi events continued for another few months. Protestors struggled to take the park back; the cops stood their ground; people from not only Istanbul but also numerous other cities in Turkey grouped, regrouped, fought, lost, and eventually gave up. 'I spent that month in the streets. But then, like many of my friends, I felt tired. The events proved to be a big intermission in our lives. But it was a necessary intermission. Thanks to it, the park became an arena for us. It became a place of meetings, where we came across different situations and realities.'

If all goes well, Yürükoğulları will graduate by the time this book is published. Not long ago he sent an application to the British Museum, where he hopes to spend a few months doing research in the field of restoration and conservation. He has watched closely the Occupy London events and is all too aware of the rising racism and anti-immigration policies in Europe. 'I don't see Europe or Britain as places of refuge', he tells me. 'If I move to London I will continue my struggle there. I feel like I am endowed with the earth, not just a particular place in it, but all of it. I might have been born and raised in London. None of that matters. Wherever I step into, becomes mine.' He turns his head towards the park, now almost invisible amid the blizzard. 'Wherever I go,' he says, 'I feel like I have to do something about it.'

While Cenk Yürükoğulları watched the sky from the silent and dark Gezi Park on that May day, Beybin Somuk was in the air, in an aeroplane on her way to the Netherlands. An animal rights campaigner, Somuk represented a new Turkish political party called Hayvan Partisi (the Animal Party) and had been invited to a workshop by two Animal Party MPs from the Dutch parliament in The Hague. Next morning, in The Hague, she had little idea about what was going on in Gezi Park; after long hours of networking and socializing with the animal welfare community, she turned on the TV in the evening and was surprised to see images of outrage and rebellion from the country she had left hours before. Scared and panicked, Somuk's first thought was that she would never be able to return to Turkey where a nationalist revolution had just taken place.

Somuk, who was 20 at the time, was instinctively suspicious of the uprising. 'To me it seemed like the uprising of middle-class Turks who had never faced political oppression in their lives', she tells me in the offices of Genç Siviller (Young Civilians), the Turkish NGO where she works as a project coordinator. A long conference table stands in front of us, and the walls are covered with posters announcing past events organized by Young Civilians. From the window I hear the dong of the bell tower of the Hagia Triada ('Holy Trinity'), Istanbul's largest Greek Orthodox shrine, erected there in 1880.

'I was watching CNN International in my hotel room,' Somuk remembers, 'and I got the impression that a civil war had just started in Turkey and that it would last for many years.' When Somuk returned to Istanbul a few days later, she was surprised to see this was not quite the case. 'It was abundantly clear that what I saw on TV was an illusion. Everything was happening around this park and when you went a bit away from it, it was easy to see how the events did not touch people's lives at all. In Anatolian cities people didn't care one bit for what happened at Gezi Park.'

I hear the sounds of the bustling Taksim from the open window as I listen to Somuk telling me about how people would be more sympathetic towards the protestors if they were the 'real outsiders' of Turkey: Armenians, Kurds, the headscarved people filling Taksim streets as we speak. Instead, all Somuk could see, when she looked at the protestors, were middle-class hipsters. 'It was a totally overrated event', Somuk says. 'The protestors really believed that the government would resign because of what they were doing in the park ... But let's imagine, for a moment, a middle-class civil servant sipping his tea in front of the TV in his house in Samsun. For him this was just a temporary nuisance, some small thing created by angry young Turks. "They are angry, but soon they will go home", the civil servant thinks. At the end of the day, protestors did go home and there was no change in government. So, the man in Samsun was proved right while the protestors in the park were proved wrong.'

Somuk never felt the urge to visit the park, a fact which I found surprising since she was 20 at the time and worked close by, a few hundred metres from Gezi. 'If they congregated there for a summer festival I would go ... of course. But to me the real question was this: do I want to spend time with nationalists carrying "We Are Mustafa Kemal's Soldiers!" banners?' Carried by young Turk nationalists who flocked to the park three days after the first environmentalist group resisted the police to clear the area, the banners Somuk refers to represented the nationalist segment of Gezi protestors, which was considerable. For many, it was thanks to the support of such young Turk nationalist groups that the uprising grew so massive and spread to different cities. Somuk, a liberal Kurd, has little sympathy for Turkish nationalists who often deny that Kurds exist at all (according to nationalists, Kurds are 'mountain Turks', having got their name from the 'kart kurt' sounds made by boots on snow – an explanation that deeply upsets Kurds).

'If Gezi continued as an environmentalist protest movement I would no doubt be there. The cutting of trees in Gezi Park would indeed disrupt the natural habitat of birds living there. If it was really an environmental movement I would doubtless go there. But I could see that young people who went there quickly came under the hegemony of particular political groups. And I told myself, "There is no place for me there, among young Turkish nationalists".'

Somuk was born on 20 September 1992 in the south-eastern city of Diyarbakır. That was also the day when Kurdish poet and journalist Musa Anter was brutally assassinated: his killer shot Anter two times in his leg, before shooting the prolific writer and thinker in his head. He then put a bullet in his heart.

Kurds who grew up in those years consider Turkish nationalism a direct threat to their existence, and Somuk is continuously aware of the danger of the denial of their identity. Unlike Yürükoğulları's parents, Somuk's family was very much involved in politics. Her father was imprisoned for four years after the 12 September 1980 military coup. A member of the Marxist–Leninist armed group TIKKO (Turkish Workers' and Peasants' Liberation Army), he served time in prisons in Mersin and Adana, was tortured in his prison cell and suffered traumas after his release.

'If you are born in Diyarbakır you don't need additional reasons to become political', Somuk tells me. 'People talk politics at home and on the street all the time. There is no way to avoid it.'

When Somuk was 12 she developed an interest in watching politicians on TV. In high school she started reading newspapers and saw more clearly how state intervention in their cultural and political identity affected Kurds. 'Diyarbakır people really know what it feels like to be oppressed by a state apparatus that has refused to acknowledge their ethnic identity for so long', Somuk says. 'This is pretty similar to what middle-class Turks at Gezi Park must have felt like. They thought that the state was intervening in their liberal lifestyles. Their politicization had the same roots as the politicization of Kurds.'

While living in Diyarbakır, Somuk felt compelled to devote herself to politics, upon witnessing inequalities that existed between her hometown and more industrialized parts of Turkey. She was irritated by what she describes as the 'harmful policies of *örgüt*', i.e. the PKK (Kurdistan Workers'

Party), the armed faction of the Kurdish political movement which controlled many facets of public life in the region. 'If you disagreed with their dominant political discourse, then you had little chance of expressing your dissenting views in public', Somuk explains. 'In Diyarbakır I did not really have a space for self-expression. We had a school magazine but it featured mainly poems and fiction. School administrators wanted to keep pupils away from politics.'

In 2010 Somuk came to Istanbul to study law at the private Yeditepe University. 'My parents were scared that I would get into trouble in a state university where political groups tend to fight a lot. So they sent me to a private college where the biggest public debate concerns whether Apple iPhone is technically superior to Samsung Galaxy.'

As an 18-year-old Kurdish girl who had just arrived in Istanbul, Somuk was surprised to find herself surrounded by secular-nationalists at the campus. 'Their political discourse was not my cup of tea', Somuk tells me. As a freshman law student more inclined towards liberalism, she preferred the discourse of the ruling conservative party over that of nationalist-progressives.

Somuk found her ideological allies in an NGO named Young Civilians. Since its foundation in 2000 the group had been one of the biggest supporters of the ruling AK Party. Established by a group of undergraduates in the meeting halls of Ankara's famously leftist ODTÜ (Middle Eastern Technical University), Young Civilians is best represented by its logo, a red Converse shoe, that stands for a relaxed, liberalized approach to Turkey's infamously serious and harsh political sphere. Famous for its humorous political activities, the group made a name for itself as a staunch critic of Turkey's state ideology. Somuk first heard about Young Civilians when the group announced its opposition to the official Youth Day celebrations held every year on 19 May in dozens of stadiums in Turkey; it was a fascist tradition, according to Young Civilians' much-discussed public statement. In 2003, a group of young soldiers expressed their fury at the suggestion of removing such ceremonies from Turkey's stadiums. This was followed by a news item in the left-nationalist daily *Cumhuriyet* whose headline, 'Young Officers Are Uneasy', became famous in the upcoming days. The yet unnamed group's motto ('Young Civilians Are Uneasy') was a reaction to this. Young Civilians are strongly despised by numerous left-wing groups and were nicknamed 'bastards of Soros' in a reference to their purportedly shadowy relationships with foreign powers. When in 2007 Young Civilians chose to protest against Republic Protests (to whose organization Yürükoğulları also objected) in front of a miniature replica of Mustafa Kemal's mausoleum in Istanbul's Miniatürk theme park, this tongue-in-cheek provocation aimed at diehard Kemalists marching in Ankara that day was harshly criticized. On May Day 2009, activists from the group climbed to the top of the Marmara Hotel (where I interviewed Yürükoğulları) to place there a banner that read 'Find The Gunmen Who Fired From Here' – a reference to the May Day organized there in 1977, where 34 people died after a gunman opened fire on protestors.

As the activities of Young Civilians became more famous, the group started attracting interest from the upper echelons of power. In 2007, one of its leaders was invited to an official state reception given by Turkey's most powerful statesman, President Abdullah Gül. Wearing a black suit and Converse shoes, the activist-guest was a curious sight at the official gathering and made headlines in the national press, mostly thanks to his rebellious shoes. In February 2015 a group of Young Civilians met Selahattin Demirtaş, the leader of the left-wing People's Democratic Party HDP (which I discuss in detail later in this chapter), to talk about politics before handing him a pair of Converse shoes. 'We use popular culture and humour to reach people', Somuk explains.

In December 2011 Somuk attended her maiden protest with the group after Turkish armed forces bombed 34 Kurdish civilians in Uludere, a town located on Turkey's border with Iraq. Mistaking smugglers for PKK militants, Turkish armed forces had made a horrific blunder that became one of the country's biggest humanitarian tragedies of the noughties. A few days after the massacre, Somuk watched her activist friends climb to the highest floor of Demirören AVM (a huge shopping mall opened on Istiklal Avenue a few months earlier as part of the neighbourhood's transformation) and throw to the pedestrians pieces of paper that bore the following message: 'What if those were bombs?' Intended to inform Istanbul's well-off residents and shoppers about the kind of atrocities going on in the eastern part of their country, the event made news in the media.

A month before I met her, Somuk travelled to Edirne, one of the first capitals of the Ottoman Empire, to stage a protest against that city's governor. Edirne houses Europe's second-biggest synagogue, built in the time of Sultan Abdul Hamid II in the late nineteenth century. The governor threatened Edirne's local Jewish population with closing down their synagogue and turning it into a museum, in an attempt to protest against 'the terroristic acts of Israel's security forces'. 'Synagogue Not Museum!' read the placard Somuk carried during the protest march. '"They" Are Our People!' read another placard which criticized the way the governor talked about Turkey's Jewish citizens as 'they'. In the eyes of Young Civilians, his stance was a betrayal against the good example set by Sultan Abdul Hamid II in the nineteenth century – Young Ottomans would probably react in a similar way, opposing this dastardly attack on the imperial Ottoman ideals of tolerance and coexistence.

In the months that led to the Gezi uprising, Somuk was happy with the state of Turkey and the policies of the governing party. 'In the past there was only the state discourse and the discourse of the PKK regarding the Kurdish issue; after 2010 there emerged a multiplicity of discourses. It was the beginning of something new', she says, pointing to how, in the spring of 2013, weeks before the events at Gezi Park started, the Turkish state started a peace initiative with the PKK called *açılım süreci*; the timing of this process and the uprising continues to make Somuk suspicious about what she sees as the large Turkish nationalist element at the heart of Gezi.

'We are undergoing a period of change,' she says, 'and such periods are always painful. When Gezi began I said to myself, "I wish this was not happening!" But after the protests ended, I understood that they were necessary. This energy had to be released, this confrontation had to be made. There was no other way for Turkey to go forward.'

After Gezi, Somuk's social life became complicated and she had awkward situations with many of her friends. Many liberal-minded supporters of the government whom she had befriended before started criticizing it for the heavy-handed way it dealt with protestors. Meanwhile, back at the campus, her nationalist friends' anger against the government grew by the day. 'People asked me why I did not attend Gezi', Somuk remembers. 'When I gave them my reasons they distanced themselves from me. Some of my friends unfollowed me on Twitter. I used to believe that friendships have nothing to do with politics, that they were all about personal feelings ... But I realize we are all political now. We look at each other in political terms. Nowadays, I am like, "if you don't like my politics and want me to stop supporting those values, why should we remain as friends any more?"'

On 28 May 2013, while Beybin Somuk was in The Hague for her Animal Party workshop and while Cenk Yürükoğulları struggled to keep his tent in Gezi, Sarphan Uzunoğlu, a young political advisor and speechwriter, was accompanying his boss, the socialist MP Sırrı Süreyya Önder, to the park. Protestors were surprised and heartened to see Turkey's extremely popular left-wing film-maker-cum-politician standing next to them in solidarity.

'Leftist friends believed that things would come to an end before the end of May', Uzunoğlu says, remembering his first day in the park. 'But then we reached 31 May and the whole world changed.' As a full-time socialist activist, Uzunoğlu had witnessed over previous years numerous internal fights among Turkish leftists. But now, he came across leftists there. He had fallen out with them not so long ago. They all took refuge from the riot police in the park. He realized this could be the beginning of what he termed an 'anticapitalist front'.

In April 2013, Uzunoğlu and a friend had organized a Digital Activism Workshop, and taught ten activist-journalists how to cover political events using streaming video platforms like Livestream and Ustream (one of the attendees, Gökhan Biçici, was brutally beaten by the riot police while trying to cover the events – luckily, his ordeal was recorded by passers-by who tried to protect him). Now, during the Gezi protests, Uzunoğlu watched activists use those techniques while covering the events.

Istanbul-based news agency Bia reported events that took place on 28 May:

> Police and dozers have left Taksim Gezi Park, one of the only remaining green spots in downtown Istanbul that is reportedly under the risk of a mall construction, as Peace and Democracy Party (BDP) deputy Sırrı Süreyya Önder [...] arrived to the construction area demanding proper deconstruction licences.
>
> A handful of protestors including deputy Önder [...] managed to leave behind the police barricade and confronted dozers. The group asked the operators to show proper documentation for their deconstruction work – a document that required approval from City Preservation Council. [...] Later on, police and dozers left the park.
>
> Deputy Sırrı Süreyya Önder made an appeal through Twitter, saying that they have stopped the dozer by standing against it. 'They can't tear down if everybody is here', he wrote.
>
> Under police supervision, the deconstruction left three trees de-rooted and a wall partially damaged.
>
> After the police withdrawal, demonstrators remained in the park, calling for another demonstration at 7 pm local time.

In the eyes of Uzunoğlu this was a moment of triumph: his boss (he refers to him as Sırrı abi – 'brother Sırrı'), in his capacity as a politician, had just turned Gezi into a visible event. 'Sırrı abi kickstarted the whole thing', Uzunoğlu tells me in a crowded cafe in Galatasaray. We are sitting a stone's throw away from the Galatasaray Square where, over the past 20 years, mothers of activists who had 'disappeared' or been 'lost' by the state's security forces have convened to demand justice; they are known as Saturday Mothers and Uzunoğlu is a fan of their tactics of remaining 'visible' with their weekly meetings since 27 May 1995.

'What Sırrı abi did was to make Gezi visible. Visibility is crucial in protests like this. In Occupy Wall Street, there were maybe 150 protestors but they were very visible. In Gezi, the media could have hidden the whole thing had it not been for Sırrı abi's arrival there. They had the power to ignore the existence of thousands of protestors, but once Sırrı abi arrived, they were forced to show what was going on. There were around 150 people in Gezi that day. Only when Sırrı abi visited did the media start paying attention.'

Uzunoğlu's ecstatic mood changed, however, in the following days. Not everyone there was a fan of his beloved Sırrı abi who was the de-facto spokesperson of Abdullah Öcalan, the imprisoned leader of the armed faction of Turkey's Kurdish movement, the PKK. Önder had been regularly visiting Öcalan, who is serving a life sentence on the island of Imrali off the coast of Marmara, over the past year; only two months earlier, during the *newroz* (spring day) celebrations on 21 March, Önder had addressed hundreds of thousands in the Kurdish city of Diyarbakır where he read Öcalan's call for disarmament and peace. 'I have brought you the message of Öcalan', Önder said, in front of a podium that carried images of the Kurdish leader. 'It is time for guns to go silent and for our armed militias to move outside Turkey's borders. This is not an end but the beginning of something new.' Now at Gezi, Önder found himself in the difficult position of a negotiator of peace who sparked protests against the same government with whom he was expected to conduct peace negotiations.

'It was either 4 or 5 June. Sırrı abi wanted to make a speech there. They did not allow him to do it. Some people wanted to create the impression that Kurds did not attend Gezi, that they had nothing to do with it. Those people were irritated to see Kurds inside the park.'

For Uzunoğlu, it was sad to see the way his boss was treated in the park where he had made such a crucial contribution to its preservation. He says the problem lay with the Stalinist, old-guard mentality among Gezi organizers who quickly took the reins of the protest movement from young, authentic demonstrators and handed it to Soviet-like committees. When he crossed the Bosphorus the following week and arrived at Yoğurtçu, a public park where protestors gathered in support of Gezi to voice similar demands, Uzunoğlu was irritated by the way old-school communists coordinated public forums. 'There should be no coordination in such forums', he opines. 'Setting up a podium is different from owning that podium. Young protestors at those parks were applauding Sırrı abi; they chanted slogans and demanded he become the president. But their voices were silenced. I think the reason had to do with Turkey's socialist movement which was getting smaller by the day in 2013. Everyone knew that the future of protests was with the political line represented by Sırrı abi.'

In the following days his disappointment only grew. 'I was no longer able to go to the forums. My wife was no longer able to go the forums. My best friends were no longer able to go to the forums.' He says 'orthodox political structures' destroyed a possible 'radical democracy experiment' in those parks. 'They set up this politburo inside the forums. They tried to pass in forums motions that were not discussed properly ... There were weird accusations against people like us.'

As a young man who had devoted his life to reading books by the likes of Antonio Negri, Michael Hardt and Pierre Bourdieu, Uzunoğlu was happy to watch people rebel and fight cops – he had done his share of fighting in previous years. But then, as the advisor of Önder and a bright young member of the Kurdish-left movement, he felt equally determined to treat the peace process with the seriousness it deserved.

Like his boss Sırrı Süreyya Önder, Sarphan Uzunoğlu (Sarphan means 'the one who masters difficulties') is not of Kurdish origin. Born in 1988 in Bursa, Turkey's fourth-biggest city in terms of population, he was raised in a very Turkish-nationalist environment. His parents, both born in 1965, had met while at university; his father came from a working-class background while his mother was raised in a middle-class environment. Until their divorce eight years previously, they had been a business couple, selling home appliances and leading a business-focused life in Bursa. In the 1990s they had become members of the Association of Young Business People (TUGIAD) and held staunchly liberal political views; they attended meetings by the pro-business group Liberal Democracy Movement (LDH) and contributed to attempts to build Bursa's first local television and its first airport.

Uzunoğlu went to high school in İnegöl, a borough of Bursa. There he discovered the difference between the city and the country for the first time in life. 'It was a very Ottomanist, right-wing environment', he tells me. 'My literature professor was an administrator of Ülkü Ocakları [the youth organization of the right-wing Turkish Nationalist Movement Party]. He adored me and I adored him back ... I

was a very good pupil who was not impressed by the nationalist rhetoric on offer.'

When he was 16, Uzunoğlu started reading works by
Trotsky. He devoted much of his time to computers and
Marxist classics. In 2001 his parents went bankrupt, following
the biggest financial crisis Turkey had ever experienced.
The economic collapse came the day after a fight between
Turkey's poet-cum-politician prime minister Bülent Ecevit
(he translated works by Tagore) and the staunchly republican
president Ahmet Necdet Sezer (the latter threw the Turkish
constitution in the former's face during a meeting). 'The
economic crisis resulted in an identity crisis for me', Uzunoğlu
tells me. 'I had always seen myself as a middle-class lad. Now
I found my lifestyle threatened by the prospect of poverty.'

It was during these same high school years that Uzunoğlu
saw how well organized Turkish nationalist *ülkücü* activists
were in school. 'They had a huge social network. They
constantly talked about current affairs. They were always
doing something.' Inspired by the energy of Turkish nationalists, Uzunoğlu searched for a similar group for himself and
found it among socialists. 'I became a socialist but I am proud
to say that I never became a militant of any organization.'

In the early 2000s, most middle-class lads around Uzunoğlu
suffered an identity crisis similar to his own. 'Our social group
consisted of secular middle-class boys and students from
Kurdish cities who did not yet define themselves as Kurds. We
were not part of the nationalist groups but somehow chose
to form an informal group.' In those years Uzunoğlu read
about the Iraq war and became a passionate supporter of the
anti-war movement. After Iraq he discovered atrocities that
took place in Bosnia. 'I wondered whether I should become
an Islamist', he remembers. Finally it was rock music that

decided the fate of his future self. He started reading rock fanzines and saw how the lyrics of his favourite rock songs shared common left-wing values.

Uzunoğlu graduated with honours from his high school and was among the 150 highest-scoring pupils (in the social studies section) of that year's university exam. He got a scholarship from a private university in İzmir, where he moved in 2006. 'I got my ears pierced the first day!' he remembers. 'I realized how restricted I had been by my social circle in Bursa.' He felt left behind intellectually and wanted to catch up with the world. The best way to do that, he found out, was to read two books every day. He opened a book at around nine and finished a second one in the wee hours of the following day. Thanks to this strict regime he managed to read all of Bertolt Brecht's works.

'When I first came to school to do my registration they made me sign a document where I had to promise that as a student I would never get involved in politics in an official capacity, i.e. that I would never become a registered member of a political party', he remembers.

In İzmir he lived in the university dormitory and shared a room with a very conservative male friend. He started frequenting the university theatre club, where he met what he calls 'libertarian-socialist members of Izmir's socialist community'. He also adapted short stories by the left-wing humorist Aziz Nesin for the stage. He read Marxist classics, developed an interest in Michael Hardt and Antonio Negri and went to lectures given by Marxist scholars. He also met members of Izmir's LGBTI community and read the works of Judith Butler. 'According to orthodox leftists of the city, I was this privileged kid from a private university. I had big differences with old-school leftists who grew revolutionary-style moustaches, wore dark green overcoats and acted like professional militants. I knew English; I started the day reading the *Guardian*; I got interested in Venezuela and started learning Spanish. I had this internationalist mindset which was my main revolutionary activity.'

Paradoxically, going to a private university strengthened Uzunoğlu's revolutionary beliefs. 'If it was not for the culture created there I would not have become an activist', he tells me. 'We had no hierarchy between professors and students, there was little bureaucracy, and the teaching staff had an open door policy.'

It was also in İzmir that Uzunoğlu first met people from Urfa who confidently called themselves Kurds. As his interest in their identity grew, he started taking classes from the political science department. Around the same time he launched a website named Jiyan ('Life' in Kurdish) with his Armenian and Kurdish friends. Together they vehemently advocated for a 'no' vote in the 2010 constitutional referendum on numerous articles in the Turkish constitution drawn up by the generals of the 1980 military coup. Uzunoğlu's group objected because the proposed changes did not include an article that acknowledged the existence of Kurds in the country.

During this time young activists working with him became opinion leaders and columnists; in the May Day celebrations of that year, he was happy to see Jiyan as a political group mentioned alongside Turkey's biggest unions in newspaper reports. Uzunoğlu's passionate activism also helped him get a column in the socialist *Evrensel* newspaper. 'Everyone loved me in those days,' he remembers, 'I was the people's favourite young socialist.' A Turkish Owen Jones would be a good way to describe Uzunoğlu's popularity.

But all of that changed in September 2011, when Uzunoğlu received a telephone call from Sırrı Süreyya Önder, a previously imprisoned (for seven years) socialist writer and film maker whose work Uzunoğlu had been following with admiration for some time. 'I have been following your work, too', Önder said. 'I want you to become my political advisor. Come to Istanbul. Let's work together!' Uzunoğlu quickly cancelled his plans to apply to a graduate programme in the UK. Seven months later, in April 2012, Önder decided to run for parliament.

By then Uzunoğlu was already seeing Önder as a father figure, admiring his benevolent attitude and his dogged determination to remain a communist in a country where communists are often locked up or discriminated against as loonies. 'I never looked at politics as a career, I just wanted to support this guy', Uzunoğlu tells me. 'He supported me to finish my graduate studies. He said: help me write speeches and I will help you.'

In June that year, Önder was elected to the parliament from Istanbul and with that Uzunoğlu's responsibilities grew. He wrote parliamentary inquiry petitions, helped Önder answer questions from journalists and became strongly integrated into the socialist-Kurdish political movement. His responsibilities ran from proof-reading Abdullah Öcalan's letter to the *Guardian* in January 2014 to writing two articles for the party's programme. 'When he offered me the job Önder said: "if you really want to change something in this country, here is your opportunity."' Uzunoğlu used the opportunity which, he later found out, came with a price.

Uzunoğlu's contributions to the leading media outlets of the Kurdish socialist movement landed him in trouble: he was questioned by the state prosecutor after being accused of spreading propaganda for Öcalan. As he became a black sheep in the left, Uzunoğlu became more strongly convinced that Marxism was useless in Turkey unless the Kurdish question was democratically solved. 'Our position inside the Kurdish movement was simple: if Kurds wants to fight, we want to fight as well. If Kurds don't want to fight, then we don't want to fight.'

The year 2012 was the most difficult for him. His girlfriend of the time used to telephone Uzunoğlu every Tuesday morning to ask whether he was arrested yet (terror arrests were made on Tuesday mornings). He lived in a very cheap apartment in the bohemian Cihangir neighbourhood, where he anxiously watched news about Kurdish activists and journalists getting arrested as part of what was known as 'KCK operations' conducted against the political arm of the PKK. Uzunoğlu's editor friend at the time, Osman Akınhay (who himself served time in prison in his youth), warned him about a prospective prison life. 'Anyone can get into prison; I did get into it, but you should not', he warned his young friend. 'Physically, you seem unfit for prison.'

During these days Uzunoğlu received lots of hate mail; multiple threats against his life appeared on Twitter; someone found the address of his mother's apartment and sent it to him as an ominous warning. There were rumours in Istanbul that a new wave of 'KCK operations' would take place soon and that Uzunoğlu's name was on the police's list. But the operation never took place and the police did not knock on his door on a Tuesday.

However, the social upheavals he was witnessing in those years assured Uzunoğlu that things were about to change in Turkey. 'The rise of the civil society, the politicization of the youth, the rise of anti-capitalist Muslims ... all of those began before Gezi', Uzunoğlu tells me. 'Actually the Gezi events began in 2011, not in 2013.' According to his analysis, the seeds of the uprising were planted when Metin Lokumcu, a retired teacher who was pepper sprayed and gassed during a protest event against the government in the Black Sea town of Hopa in 2011, died of a heart attack during the events.

'Hopa is the heart of Turkey's leftist movements', Uzunoğlu explains. 'When Lokumcu died that day, every leftist knew that things would be different from then on. For the first time Turkish leftists feared for their own existence. They were like, "This is not confined to Kurds and Armenians any more! Now they are coming after Turks, too!"'

Arrests of two leading leftist figures, the publisher Ragıp Zarakolu and the academic Büşra Ersanlı, were similarly fatal blows. A third factor, according to Uzunoğlu, was the hydro-electric power plants (known as HES) planned to be built in numerous cities in the Black Sea region. With support from organizations like Greenpeace, locals organized protests against the construction plans. 'Those were crucial steps that paved the way for Gezi', Uzunoğlu says.

So how come the government was not toppled by the uprising, I ask Uzunoğlu as we near the end of our meeting at Galatasaray. 'Well, all the factors were there; the economic foundations for a revolution were there. I was interviewed by Italian television during Gezi. I said "at the moment, there is no political entity in power in Turkey". After the interview I came to the realization that one needs a power since you can only replace one political power with another.' Another realization was that something as essential as the Kurdish peace process needed an interlocutor to be able to continue.

Here he was, divided between his socialist and supporter-of-Kurdish-rights roles. Uzunoğlu had to decide whether a revolution was more favourable to the peace process. He smiles while talking about this process; his expression is a characteristic mixture of passionate activism and political calculation. Here is an angry young Turk who knows the value of passion and dissent, as well as the necessity of formal political processes. 'If you have a problem as big as the Kurdish question in your country and if that problem is being resolved,' Uzunoğlu says, 'toppling the government, through whose cooperation that problem is solved, may not be the best thing to do.'

On 7 June 2013, two weeks into the Gezi uprising, Turkey's prime minister Recep Tayyip Erdoğan returned to Istanbul from a two-week state tour of North Africa. Erdoğan's plane was scheduled to land in Istanbul at around midnight that day; for his supporters this was an excellent occasion to show him their continuing support. For Mehmet Alğan, a 27-year-old activist who had no previous formal ties to Erdoğan's party, it proved to be the night that changed his life beyond return.

For Alğan, the night began with a crucial decision: if he chose to go to Istanbul's Atatürk Airport to welcome the prime minister, that would mean one thing; if not, something quite different. Tens of thousands went there that night to greet Erdoğan, who gave a defiant speech, promising to treat the protestors in a civil way; but he also made sure that everyone understood how he was not changing the position of his government one bit. 'Just give us the order, we will go and destroy the *çapulcu* in Gezi Park!' a small group of his supporters chanted. To the absolute shock of many watching the event on TV from their beds or living rooms that night,

Erdoğan did little to counter that sentiment either. He knew that thanks to this event, broadcast live on every television channel, his party and supporters were giving a clear message that he desperately needed: the conservatives were here to stay. He was also kickstarting a new phase in his political career. He would now be the representative of the 'Strong Will' ('Sağlam İrade'), the personification of the self-assured and defiant will of Turkey's nation.

'Going to greet him relieved me', Alğan remembers, sitting alongside his fiancée in a busy restaurant about two years after that consequential night. This is a hard-earned interview for which Alğan spared time during his busy political campaign to be elected as an AK Party MP from the southeastern city of İskenderun. 'There were absurd figures in the crowd: some people came there with their shrouds to show they were ready to die for Erdoğan', Alğan says. 'But then again, those people who came to greet the prime minister constituted this group where I could easily feel at home, so I didn't mind.'

Alğan remembers getting into the subway at around 11 p.m. that evening alongside two female friends. 'All the trains were incredibly crowded. I was able to move through the crowd thanks to my female friends; many Erdoğan supporters give way when they see headscarved women, telling them things like "geç bacım" [go ahead, sister]. Moments after we became part of the big group, Tayyip Erdoğan started to speak. He gave an excellent speech. It felt like all the tension that was built up in us was gone. Our defensive approach about the protests suddenly changed; in the previous two weeks we felt like the Gezi people were our moral superiors, that they purportedly had moral superiority; now it felt like the opposite was the case. That night we came to our own and this is how I started feeling like a part of Erdoğan's party.'

In the past Alğan was irritated by the idea of belonging to a big crowd. He had been involved in political activism for as long as he could remember, but was never a card-carrying member of an established political party. 'That night at the airport I made peace with the conservative sociology to which I belonged. For me it would be more difficult not to go and greet Tayyip Erdoğan. If I watched his arrival on the TV in my apartment, that night would be more difficult for me. I wanted to express my feelings there and then. I wanted to feel like a part of a story. Going there was the best way to achieve these things.'

Alğan had come a long way to reach that moment. Born in 1986 in Lebanon, he had often felt like an outsider in Turkey. His father, who was born in the Turkish city of Mardin, had moved to Lebanon in his youth. 'In the 1950s and 1960s when most families migrated to Istanbul, Arabs from Mardin chose to move to Beirut which was known as the Paris of the Middle East', Alğan says. 'Those families knew the Arabic language and took advantage of it.' During the Lebanese Civil War (1975–90) Alğan's father stayed in Beirut while his wife and family returned to Turkey. (Alğan is the sixth of seven children. His father decided to return to Turkey many years later, after his retirement; he moved back to İskenderun from Beirut, two months before Alğan announced the start of his electoral campaign in 2015.)

Once in Turkey, the family moved to İskenderun, a city that was economically more advantageous. There Alğan grew up in the district of Kocatepe, a poor neighbourhood whose residents have frequently made the decision to migrate to Istanbul in subsequent years. At high school Alğan met pupils coming from Alawite, Christian, Turkmen and Roma backgrounds. He remembers the day Turkish president

Turgut Özal died in 1993, an event that upset him for slightly unpolitical reasons. 'I couldn't watch my beloved cartoons any more!' Alğan remembers. 'I was crying in the living room all day long. I asked my parents what all the fuss was about and why all television programmes were about Özal. I just couldn't understand why they were not showing my beloved cartoons any more.'

In high school Alğan developed an interest in politics. He learned about Kemalism, Turkey's founding ideology, and became an admirer of Mustafa Kemal Atatürk. 'There was this photograph of Mustafa Kemal that showed him stretching his hand out of a train compartment to greet a citizen. This photographed showed his civil side; I remember putting the photograph on my wall in İskenderun.'

His parents were not big readers; they did not buy newspapers. He was the first Alğan to become a devoted reader. He was also the first to become a leftist. 'I had this strong sense of justice', he remembers. 'I used to see all those inequalities in İskenderun where you see on the streets very poor people as well as the rich.' Although his family background is quite conservative, Alğan's uncles and grandparents had taken part in strikes, as had many Arab Sunni workers. So he saw nothing wrong in becoming an activist as the son of a conservative family. 'I had this rebellious spirit in me. When I went downtown I saw all these people who were better dressed than I was. I realized that I was part of İskenderun's poor. This helped me grow a sense of dissent in my soul.'

In high school Alğan set up a student organization. He read texts by Deniz Gezmiş, the legendary Turkish revolutionary; he heard people speak about Marx's *Capital* but realized that none of them had actually read the book. It was around this time he started having problems with his friends at the leftist organization. 'We had this disagreement about smoking in the toilets. My friends talked about changing the world while secretly smoking in the school toilets. One day I said: "People who are meant to listen to you don't care for what you say precisely because your revolutionary speeches take place in these toilets! They see you as men-secretly-smoking-cigarettes-in-the-loo."' Alğan's concern for the group's self-image today sounds like excellent advice. But his friends begged to differ; after listening to Alğan's critique, they informed him that he was no longer welcome at their meetings.

'Right from the beginning I demanded what was possible. I told friends: let's *imagine* the impossible while *demanding* the possible. Let's not talk about "one day" but instead talk about "today"', Alğan says, showing how his transformation into a young man fully devoted to politics began during that time. 'Big ideologies that talk about big things about the future failed to convince me ... I was more interested in making things better gradually, day by day.'

A few weeks before Hrant Dink was assassinated, Alğan decided to send him an e-mail. 'In my draft I advised him to stay silent for a while ... Thanks to the way mainstream media had portrayed him, some people were infuriated with Dink's opinions; I saw him on TV and he looked so tired and depressed. I was devastated to see what was being done to this kind, kind man. I read his piece where he talked about feeling like an anxious dove. But then I said to myself, "why should Hrant Dink care for the views of this kid from İskenderun?"'

On the day of Dink's funeral, attended by more than a hundred thousand people in Istanbul, Alğan felt he had to do something. So he bought the only copy of Dink's newspaper *Agos* in İskenderun and left his house to start a long walk in the city, imagining this as Dink's funeral march. 'I walked downtown and back. When I returned home, my eyes were filled with tears', he remembers.

In his last year at high school Alğan decided to go to Istanbul for college. 'I wanted to swim in a bigger lake', he tells me. He studied Turkish literature at college but was deeply disappointed by the programme. 'All the courses were about old Turkish and very ancient variations of the language, instead of modern literature, as I imagined.' On campus he didn't have many friends, a situation he explains by his comparably advanced age when he enrolled on the programme. 'All the pupils were three years my junior. There was a very apolitical atmosphere inside the campus. I was so full of ambition and had so many big goals: I wanted to meet new, mature people and read more books, watch more films ... Most of my fellow pupils only dreamed about becoming teachers. I dreamed about changing the country.'

In the increasingly political environment of Istanbul he befriended leftists and Kurdish activists as well as liberal Young Civilians campaigners. In 2011 he suddenly found his political focus during the Syrian uprising against that country's rulers. Alğan was among the founders of an NGO called Nahda ('enlightenment' in Arabic) for which he became one of the chief conference organizers.

'I was always interested in foreign policy and Middle Eastern issues', he remembers. 'I am Lebanon-born, so it is my region. As someone who spent his youth on the border checkpoints in order to meet relatives during holidays, I know an awful lot about borders. After the Arab Spring began in 2011, I spent all my energy on organizing conferences and meetings here in Istanbul where I invited activists from the region.'

For members of Nahda, the toppling of Hosni Mubarak was the real instigator of the Arab Spring. Once the uprisings spread to Syria, Alğan and fellow Nahda members started educating Syrian activists. They taught them accelerated courses on using social media, as well as providing them with logistics. 'We gave them laptops and cameras', Alğan recalls. 'Our goal was simple: to help Syrians build a government that would express people's political views better than they currently did. What people in Syria asked for was a life where the majority of people could express themselves in a better, more honourable, more prosperous way.'

In the eyes of Alğan, the plight of Syrians bore inescapable similarities to people in Turkey. 'Here the ruling party helped people who had previously been excluded from power by Turkey's founding ideology. Our government gave people the necessary tools to express themselves in a better way. What made Turkey different from Syria was the former's closeness to the Western bloc. When a group of generals organized a coup in Turkey they had to give up that political power after a while. Poor Syrians did not have this chance because their state was part of the Soviet bloc. Once they made their coups, those generals could remain in power for many years. In Turkey we had polling stations and elections; we wanted Syrians to have the same instruments.'

The developments he had witnessed in Syria and Egypt led Alğan to believe in the importance of rebelling against tyrannies as well as defending the legitimacy of democratically elected governments. 'One needs to march on the streets to protect the ruling party if need be', he says.

This was why, during 2013's uprising in Gezi, Alğan was led to draw a parallel between Turkey, Egypt and Syria. 'I totally empathize with the anger of protestors who felt they could not express themselves in public and decided to use the Gezi events as a platform for that', he tells me. 'But there was this argument used during the events that I would never agree with. "The ballot box is not everything", according to this line of thought. To me, this is actually a confession of people whose real thought is this: "We can't beat you in the ballot box, so we will use our only remaining option and try to get rid of you by going out on the streets!" To this, my answer is: "Hey, wait a minute. Of course I agree that we need a stronger civil society and the need for democratic institutions and all that ... Let's discuss all these issues but do that using the formal channels of democracy." When I hear people say things like democracy should take place on streets, I feel sceptical. Look at what happened in Egypt. People marched on the streets against Morsi, which is true; but then they said 22 million signatures were collected against him, which was a total sham. What happened in Egypt resembled what happened in 1950s Turkey very closely. Here the leader of the Democrat Party, Adnan Menderes, was ousted by generals who then hanged him. To legitimize this, generals had used newspaper stories about Menderes sending Turkish youths to "meat machines" where he tore them to pieces.'

Alğan says he has nothing against people marching on the streets. 'But protests are actually better when you want to get rid of a dictator, like Mubarak in Egypt. When you have a democratically elected president, then trying to topple him on the street has little meaning. A dictator is a political figure who gives no chance to his people but to march on the streets. When you use this same technique against a democratically elected government ... this is where the problems begin.'

Despite his reservations against and disagreements with Gezi protestors, Alğan stayed in the park for a long time so as to be able to observe young people, like Cenk Yürükoğulları, who pitched tents there and stood their ground for weeks. As a prospective politician, he wished to find out what those young people really wanted. 'The language of the state apparatus is harsh', Alğan admits. 'The state has no conscience. The state is blind to the kind of little personal stories we hear about in public. Civil society brings a breath of fresh air to that cold mentality of the state apparatus. But then the actions of civil society must go hand in hand with the ballot box and democratic elections – those things are indispensable.'

Alğan's phone rings. In less than an hour he has to be in a television studio for a discussion programme about the upcoming elections. He says he needs to hit the road. Before leaving me in the restaurant, he completes his point about the importance of elections. 'Those young people wanted to express themselves', he says, referring to the protestors. 'But then the ballot box is the best way invented by humans to express their political choices. We have yet to find a better way of self-expression and so should value what we have.' And with that, he disappears into the crowd.

Those young activists who have been so effectively defining Turkey's political sphere in the past few years as parliamentarians, political advisors and campaign managers resemble very closely their reformist-minded ancestors from the late nineteenth and early twentieth centuries. While talking to them, I remembered how the first thing to know about the historical phenomenon of 'Young Turks' is that there is not one Young Turk, but many, and that this has long been the case.

Turkish historian Şerif Mardin, who penned the definitive account of the subject in *The Genesis of Young Ottoman Thought*, lists five different versions of *jeune Turks*. The term was first used by Charles MacFarlane, a Scottish traveller, in 1827. MacFarlane wrote about how an admiration for the military, which at the time was undergoing modernization, was 'pretty generally shared by the young Turks'. The term originally referred to a new generation of Ottoman citizens who looked up to members of the Ottoman army, whose transformation into a Western-style organization they considered an important feat for the empire. Nevertheless, MacFarlane's observations gave but a brief glimpse of the political spirit that would irreversibly transform the country, continuing to be influential more than a century later. As Mardin shows, the term existed in a cloud of ambiguity at the time and referred to both modernizers and their conservative-minded critics:

Mention of the term 'Jeune Turquie' may be found as early as 1855 in Ubicini's *La Turquie Actuelle*. Even at that time, however, Ubicini found the term 'Jeune Turquie' too ambiguous and proposed the distinction of 'Jeune Turquie de Mahmoud' and 'Jeune Turquie d'Abdul Medjid'. By the first term Ubicini attempted to characterize the conservative-reformist trend. He stated that the second group, on the other hand, was so Europeanized that it would have been immaterial, whether it had taken its ideas from the Koran or the Gospels, but that it believed in neither.

In other words, the division among young Turks began as soon as the term was invented: one of its paths led to conservative lands, the other to progressive ones. The confusion about the distinction between conservative-reformist and European-minded progressive Young Turks played an important role in Western representations of Turkey. The appearance of the first two 'young Turk' characters above were followed by 'a third Young Turkey', a secret political organization named 'the Patriotic Alliance' which was intent on 'combating the very tendencies of the over-westernized Jeune Turquie of Abdul Medjid of which Ubicini spoke'.

That the first properly modern dissident movement in Ottoman political history had a pan-Islamist agenda comes as surprising news and is an often overlooked detail of Ottoman history. Young Ottomans' pan-Islamic political agenda was quite sophisticated and had little in common with the more reactionary groups who prepared for an Islamic holy war. Mardin lists 'the Young Ottomans' lack of aggressive proclivities, their emphasis on self-improvement through the adoption of selected features of Western life, the purely defensive stand involved in their demands that Western slights on Ottoman sovereignty cease' as chief features of their ideology.

Young Ottomans wanted to reform the Ottoman state through constitutionalism and a return to the principles of Islam and shari'a law. They managed to produce a synthesis between Enlightenment ideas and Islam. The egalitarianism endorsed by Young Ottomans also had an anti-Christian ring, since the centralized, Europe-minded reforms they opposed gave privileges to Christian populations which, they argued, resulted in Muslims feeling underprivileged. Because the empire's Westernization gave its Christian subjects a privileged status, and reshaped the state apparatus through Westernized institutions, Young Ottomans proposed either to do away with those privileges or to redefine the concept of 'Ottoman nation' in such a way that the Muslim citizens didn't feel offended by the reforms.

A common hatred for the rule of Westernizers of the time, as well as 'a belief that by constitutional and representative government more could be done than these Ottoman statesmen had achieved', brought Young Ottomans together. Like modern-day young conservatives who use social media websites such as Twitter and Facebook to get across their views on political events, the 1870s generation of Young Ottomans had an urgent desire to express their opinions and a deep wish to keep the empire united against the tutelage and interventionism of foreign powers, while propagating a politics of worldwide Islamic union. An important quality they shared was a total devotion to the Ottoman state – they never wanted to revolutionize or replace the state apparatus but to fix it, so that it could function as it did in its days of glory.

The kind of tyranny Young Ottomans fought against is little known in contemporary Turkey and would, if they knew it, surprise many. Young Ottomans never questioned the sultanate or the monarchy, and directed all their energies to countering the policies of the Sublime Porte which they perceived as the centre of the empire's doomed Westernization process and a stifling process of bureaucratic centralization (Westernization and bureaucracy are arguably the two main antagonists of Turkey's modern-day conservatives). Although they did not view the Ottoman sultan as a tyrant, Young Ottomans did use the concept of tyranny and opposed it, in relation to modern-izers whose policies they perceived as running counter to 'the great opportunities afforded by the "unfathomable sea of the Şeriat"'. Young Ottomans despised the tyranny of the super-fluous, the efficient but soulless invention imported from the West. They accused the Westernizing bureaucrats of having adopted the most superficial parts of European culture, those aspects which the Young Ottomans considered immoral. One of their complaints, for example, was that Westernization had been understood by Fuad Paşa and his imitators as equivalent to 'the establishment of theatres, frequenting ballrooms, being liberal about the infidelities of one's wife and using European toilets'. Again, Namık Kemal stated that he rejected a Europeanization which consisted of letting women walk around décolleté.

Like modern-day conservative-reformist-minded supporters of the AK Party, Young Ottomans saw the transformation of the state apparatus using efficiency as the central aim as being detrimental to the Islamic foundations of the empire. They believed that the dominance of Westernization-obsessed bureaucracy resulted 'in an ideological vacuum, for the Tanzimat statesmen contributed nothing to replace the Şeriat as a measuring rod of good and evil in politics. They did not realize the implications of the creation of such an ideological vacuum. They were Europeanized to the extent of accepting Islam as a "private" religion.' In what may seem to us today like a historical irony, it was the perceived destruction of shari'a law through Westernization that first gave way to dissent in the Ottoman Empire, whose ideological continuity proved long-lasting and is crucial to understanding the mindset of Turkey's conservative youth.

If Young Ottomans are the ideological forefathers of Turkey's conservative reformers, the much better-known Young Turks, founders of the Committee of Union and Progress (CUP), are behind some of the politics of today's secular-progressive movement. Although the movement had its roots in the Ottoman military, the political concept associated with its name, *İttihadçılık* ('Unionism') refers today to a political stance that endorses Enlightenment values of fraternity, equality and freedom, imposing them on society through revolutions and sometimes coups, instead of the traditional processes of representative democracy.

The crucial political event that led Young Turks to form the Committee of Union and Progress was Sultan Abdul Hamid II's increasingly erratic and autocratic rule, culminating in his abrupt decision to close down the first Ottoman parliament in 1878, which marked the end of the First Constitutional Era that had begun two years previously. The Constitutional Era had been the crowning success of Young Ottomans, since it was their members who had penned *Kanûn-u Esâsî* (Basic Law) of 1876, the first constitution of the empire, with which their activities came to a halt.

Young Turks were politically much more ambitious than their conservative forefathers in that they were ready to use any means necessary to force Ottoman Sultan Abdul Hamid II to readopt the constitution and bring an end to his arbitrary rule. This they achieved in 1908 through the Young Turk Revolution, which reversed the sultan's suspension of parliament and kickstarted the Second Constitutional Era of the empire.

While Young Ottomans was made up of a group of high-level bureaucrats working at the Sublime Porte, Young Turks was a middle-class movement that found support from a wide range of social classes. The Istanbul correspondent of *The Times* described their supporters in the following way: 'The high officials, generally speaking,' he wrote, 'were hostile to the movement ... The lower classes ... were, as a rule, indifferent. It was among the junior officers of the army and navy, the middle and lower grades of the civil service, the professional classes, and the *ülema*, that the movement for reform carried all before it.' The collaboration of nationalists, secularists, Armenians, Greeks and different segments of Ottoman society, under the Young Turk banner, has been a clear model for modern-day protestors. While this historical collaboration of different Ottoman subjects is best explained by the bad feeling toward Abdul Hamid II's arbitrary and autocratic rule, the modern-day union of opposition forces in Turkey can be explained by a similar urge to fight what is seen by some as a repressive administration.

The Young Ottoman movement, although secretive like Young Turks, never resorted to the use of force and was a strong defender of the sultanate; Young Turks, in contrast, evolved into a political movement that terrified the palace through its systematic and influential assassinations of those loyal to the sultan. Once it assumed power in 1908, the Young Turks' Committee of Union and Progress found itself unready to govern the empire whose political machinations it had fought to control for so long. Not accepting political responsibility for the empire's government, Young Turks initially fulfilled the function of a checks and balances mechanism, making sure the sultan stayed true to his commitments about constitutional rule.

The clash between those seemingly irreconcilable visions attests to historical continuities between the Young Ottoman and Young Turk movements. It reminds us how Turkey's civil society gathers its cultural and political energy from the antagonism between those century-old rivals.

Young Turks and Young Ottomans survive in modern-day Turkey. Despite hurried analyses of the political unrest in Turkey that describe it as a fight between a monolithic group of young activists and a repressive system supported by ignorant masses who should know better, the real dynamic of unrest among Turkey's furious youth exists between these equally influential and long-lasting historico-political positions.

❋

On 8 June 2015, three months after I interviewed him, Mehmet Alğan was elected as an MP for İskenderun. The governing party, the latest incarnation of the Young Ottoman spirit, won a little more than 40 per cent of the vote and although triumphant, suffered an almost 10 per cent drop in its share. With these results, 2015's general elections which so deeply changed Alğan's life prompted a new era in Turkey's politics. According to political analysts, the youth had voted away from the governing AK Party: this led to the rise of two parties, the Kurdish-leftist HDP and the Turkish-nationalist MHP (the latter's share rose to 16.3 per cent from 13 per cent in 2011, an increase of around two million votes). Sarphan Uzunoğlu's socialist boss, Sırrı Süreyya Önder, entered parliament thanks to his party HDP's unexpected (and unprecedented for a Kurdish-leftist party) 13 per cent vote. A month after the elections Uzunoğlu told me he was moving away from politics and focusing more on academia: 'I had done my bit for the people', he said, referring to HDP's electoral success.

Despite HDP's gains in the election, conservatives continue to be in power, but their activists are not exactly upset by the AK Party becoming the first party in the elections. The electoral losses meant that the kind of Young Ottoman approach represented by the AK Party (religion-centred, entrepreneurial, conservative-minded and constitution-alist) had taken a blow, accompanied by a fascinating new phenomenon: the reawakening of the 'Young Turk' spirit – the monarch-defying, establishment-challenging approach that was behind the foundation of the Turkish republic – albeit under the umbrella of a Kurdish party and in the form of a politics of environmentalist-socialism, rather than Turkish republicanism. Of course, MHP's 16.3 per cent vote meant that the Turkish nationalist vote, too, was also on the rise.

According to Turkish newspapers, the gains of MHP and HDP were due to first-time voters and the youth in general, who favoured the Young Turk spirit over the Young Ottoman. But their triumph proved short-lived: not able to form a coalition over the summer, this reborn Young Turk spirit would lose its momentum in the snap elections on 1 November, when the inheritors of the Young Ottoman mindset would win nearly 50 per cent of the vote – their biggest electoral win ever.

The week before the general elections, Beybin Somuk graduated from law school. When I texted her after the elections she was on her way to become a lawyer, getting ready to apply to law firms. At Young Civilians she continues to work on her project, The World is Bigger Than Five, which attempts to build 'a functioning and democratic United Nations crucial in solving international conflicts that threaten the lives of millions' and calls for 'the removal of the veto right of the permanent members of United Nations Security Council'. Hers are big dreams which received much media attention after Erdoğan endorsed the project in a public speech.

After his long run from Gezi Park to the adjoining Maçka Park on the day of the police raid, Cenk Yürükoğulları joined the resistance movement against the destruction of the market gardens of Istanbul's Yedikule district. When I last spoke to him, he was in a purgatorial mood: his application to the British Museum had been rejected. He had made up his mind to go to Rome, where he wants to work on how to properly restore historical monuments and conserve nature. This was his last year at college and he wanted to arrange a way out of Turkey before his studentship expired. He had hitchhiked his way through Russia a few years ago. If Yürükoğulları manages to get a visa and buy a ticket to Rome, it will be the first time this angry young Turk will ever set foot in Europe.

# CHAPTER TWO

# Turkish Rebellion
# as a Fine Art

In Turkey, artists are admired and feared in equal measure. *'Kızı gönlüne bırakırsan ya davulcuya varır, ya zurnacıya'* is an idiom universally known in the country: if you allow your daughter to act as her heart desires, she will wed either a drummer or a horn player. This is intended as a warning. Not unlike young people's attraction to rebellious, politically engaged schoolmates at college, there is a certain attractive air around the practitioners of the artistic life, thanks to the excitement that life is thought to contain. Poets, painters, film makers, curators and novelists are the ones who can speak truth to power, after all, and that is an exciting proposition. In Turkey, speaking truth to power has always come with a heavy price. Over the course of the twentieth century, only a few Turkish poets or novelists worthy of the name managed to escape the fury of the state apparatus. Numberless novels, short stories, poems and films have picked prison life as their subject. Their creators, after all, had experienced prison life at first hand: from the poet Nazım Hikmet to the novelist Orhan Kemal and the film maker Yılmaz Güney, Turkey's leading artists have been all too familiar with the repressive nature of the Turkish state.

Gezi Park, where the uprising of 2013 began, is located in Taksim, a square that stands at the intersection of neighbourhoods which host Istanbul's artistic community. Interestingly, most of the artists who flocked to the park were the beneficiaries of the system built in the past three decades.

Until the liberalization of Turkey's economy was kickstarted in the 1980s, the country's art scene was dominated by state institutions. There were numerous, well-funded, influential state conservatories, academies, and official film and literature institutions that helped forge a cultural scene where the typical artist or culture figure was a civil servant and a staunch defender of the Turkish state's secular-nationalist foundations.

When that changed in the years surrounding the end of the Cold War, artists started to play a different role. Turkey's fast-paced liberalization transformed the institutional structure of the art world and resulted in the rise of small galleries and privately owned art museums. Sponsorship from financial institutions and major corporations meant that artists could lead more privileged lives and achieve an international reach. With the rise of contemporary art and post-modern, post-colonial literary figures, the once docile, state-friendly artists and authors became the gravediggers of Turkey's state apparatus.

Two politicians contributed most to this new state of affairs. From 1983 to 1993, Turgut Özal was the incarnation of liberal conservatism: as prime minister and president he privatized previously public cultural institutions. From the early 2000s onwards, Recep Tayyip Erdoğan played a similar role: as prime minister and president he strongly supported the privatization of the artistic sphere. Özal and Erdoğan both struggled to keep the artistic world separate from the state, and to the older generation of artists this did not come as welcome news. Anger in the theatre world was especially high, since most of the actors who worked as civil servants in public theatres now needed to enter the wild, unruly world of private entertainment.

A similar atmosphere of change spread upon poets and novelists who found themselves in Turkey's new literary scene, which was more and more defined by market forces. In this new world, young writers became increasingly individualistic but also played a more rebellious, social role. Thanks to their large followings on social media sites like Twitter, they were able to incite their fans to rebellion.

If protests were energized by Istanbul's artistic community who lived and worked around Gezi Park, it was thanks to the rise of a new, freelance class of artists and cultural operators who had no fear of the state, whose interests they were no longer obliged to defend.

As for inspiration, the uprisings can't truly be said to have inspired a great novel, film or poem – that has not happened yet. But in this new spirit of ambiguity and change, film makers, artists and poets alike felt amused, and that feeling they paradoxically owed to the violent transformation of Turkey's cultural world.

In September 2013, more than two months after the Gezi uprising was suppressed by riot police, Turkey's young protestors re-emerged. They caught the attention of cops and the media with artful new ways of protesting: a so-called Standing Man appeared in front of a cultural centre overlooking the park and just stood there, for eight hours, while more than 300 people joined him in standing still and refusing to leave the square, asking cops if it was now a crime to stand up. Erdem Gündüz, the young performer who started this act (he later confessed to thinking about the legacy of Mustafa Kemal Atatürk while staring at the huge Turkish flag on the cultural centre), was the perfect personification of how artists and protestors could inspire one another. With such collaborations in preparation, the Turkish state found it increasingly difficult to keep Turkey's youth in order. This time it seemed as if they were everywhere: in numerous cities in Turkey's Anatolian heartland, millennials took to the streets and, before long, realized that the police were quite prepared for such confrontations.

On 10 September, a group of young protestors marched in Antakya, a province of the border town Hatay. A young man named Ahmet Atakan joined protestors as they shouted slogans against Ankara's mayor Melih Gökçek, whose plan to build a road through the campus of ODTU (Middle Eastern Technical University) in Ankara was fiercely opposed by the university's famously radical left-leaning students. Then, at around 2 a.m. that morning, Atakan was found dead on the street.

'Witnesses and activists claimed that Atakan was allegedly hit in the head by a gas canister fired by the police', ran *Hurriyet Daily News*'s report on how Atakan was killed. 'However, the police released a statement saying that footage from a local police camera showed that Atakan fell from a building, and that no intervention by the police was visible. "It can be understood from the examination of the voice and images of the footage belonging to a police camera that was made public that no intervention took place from the police vehicles toward the attackers, either before or at the time of the fall of the person [Ahmet Atakan]", the statement said.' For some this explanation was sufficient, while others did not believe it one bit.

On the morning of this young man's death, angry young Turks took to the streets, with an impassioned attempt to express their fury and frustration. Atakan's death had come after the death of five others during the summer riots of 2013. All of the deceased were young male protestors. Ethem Sarısülük was 26 years old; Abdullah Cömert, 22; Mehmet Ayvalıtaş, 20; Ali İsmail Korkmaz, 19, and Medeni Yıldırım, 18. Ahmet Atakan was 22. During the events that led to his death, a police officer named Mustafa Sarı died in similarly tragic conditions, after falling from a bridge while trying to arrest a protestor. Sarı, too, was a young man when he died at the age of 27.

In the hours following Atakan's death, a 22-year-old poet named Aytuğ Akdoğan was on his way to Kadıköy, the Anatolian neighbourhood of Istanbul that had in the previous days staged violent confrontations between riot police and protestors supportive of the uprising in Ankara.

It was 6 a.m. when Akdoğan arrived in Kadıköy. 'Tear gas was everywhere. Total chaos. I couldn't see anything', Akdoğan tells me in a cafe overlooking the Galata Kulesi ('the tower of Christ'), a medieval stone tower built in 1348 by the Genoise. He is chain-smoking and speaking in short sentences, in a deep voice.

'Nothing could be discerned among the fog. I saw a group of cops running on the street where I walked. Then I started to escape from them. There were maybe 20 people. Maybe 30. They came after and arrested me.'

Akdoğan had travelled to Kadıköy to meet his publisher, but instead of talking with him, ended up in a police van that took him to the police headquarters. There, a solicitor appointed by the bar advised him to use his right to remain silent. From there he was carried to a state hospital for medical checks. Luckily his friends knew about Akdoğan's ordeal.

'Moments after they arrested me I sent a tweet. "Handcuffed, I am being taken away." Around 200 people shared it. Some made fun of me. They asked how on earth I managed to tweet when I was handcuffed.' His hands were placed in front of his body and this was how he could use his phone, Akdoğan explains to me.

As he was being taken to the police station, Akdoğan was extremely anxious about what would now happen to him. From his cell in the station he watched the sunrise and listened to the muezzin of a nearby mosque chant the morning prayer. 'I was watching the scene behind bars. I had this big concern about the possibility of being tortured by cops. There were ominous rumours about police stations, how protestors somehow associated with the Gezi uprising were mistreated there. I was afraid to become one of the tortured ones.'

After spending 12 hours there, Akdoğan was finally released, but this was not the end of the matter. His lawyer informed Akdoğan about a possible court case on the horizon, thanks to which the young man found himself in a very uncomfortable situation. 'That totally fucked up my psychology', he tells me, lighting a cigarette. 'According to the legislation, if you get arrested twice for the same crime, you end up in prison. End of story. I had this fear of getting arrested in public and horrible panic attacks. For a while I could not step onto the streets again. Whenever I saw a cop with his uniform and helmet from afar, I was reminded of the cop who took me into custody. And I started thinking about what happened to all the people who really *did* things to the police. If they treated me, this young guy who had done absolutely nothing, in this manner, what would they do to others?'

Akdoğan's court case continued for a year and a half, during which time he had to go to the court in Istanbul's Kartal neighbourhood numerous times. 'My lawyer said there was no need for me to come', Akdoğan tells me. 'But, you see, I was obsessed with the whole thing.'

It is not at all surprising that this young man who fashions himself as a Turkish incarnation of the beatnik spirit, through his poetry and novels, was born on the road. In 1992, Akdoğan's mother gave birth to him in Kocaeli, many miles away from her and her husband's hometown Erzincan. Theirs is the tale of a classic soldier family: Akdoğan's father, a retired military officer, brought his family to different cities in Anatolia; from Kars to Malatya, Akdoğan spent his childhood on the road, growing up in military lodgings, surrounded by career officers and their relatives. He remembers those years affectionately and describes his childhood as 'problem-free'. Once Akdoğan's family moved to Istanbul during his last year in high school, however, things began to change.

During classes at school Akdoğan started having anger management issues. 'I just couldn't control my temper', he tells me. 'I used to get involved in all kinds of fights. My parents were concerned that I would start up a gang. They knew that I had problems with authority.' Akdoğan was sent to a private college, where he got into fights with fellow pupils and was forced to change his programme after failing seven classes in one semester. 'My parents were summoned to the school', Akdoğan remembers. 'They were asked why I was such an unruly child.'

I ask him why he picked fights with his fellow pupils, as if I was his high school advisor. 'Perhaps I was in the wrong but I just couldn't help it. I overreacted to things one could very easily forgive. With my professors I had this big problem about hierarchy. They were good professors but when I was an adolescent I believed that nobody could teach me anything. I wanted to destroy the hierarchy between them and us. So I rebelled. Whenever they wanted to teach me something, I was like, hey, I don't need that information *at all*.'

Both of Akdoğan's parents are retired: he from the military, she from a big Turkish bank. He has an elder brother who works in finance, and has a good income as a broker. With such high standards and demands in mind, his parents were devastated to see their young son become so bitter and angry about life. Akdoğan had continuous academic problems which went hand in hand with his lack of friends. When your family moves from one Anatolian city to another every two years, it is hard to keep friends, he tells me.

'I remember standing by the window and watching my parents cry in front of the school. I had no desire to learn anything when I went to class. All that changed when I moved on to college, where I came into contact with stuff that really interested me.'

Akdoğan was a big fan of the American writer Charles Bukowski, whose life philosophy he made his own. 'I liked his impervious attitude. I liked the way he looked at things, how he was aware of everything and how he did absolutely nothing about them.' Akdoğan also discovered writers like Jean-Paul Sartre and Allen Ginsberg, whose approach to literature he would later attempt to adapt to his own writing. 'But I always preferred Bukowski's apolitical stance over theirs', he says. 'My only connection to life was literature in those days.

Until 28 May 2013, the day on which everything changed in Turkey, I had not once bought a political magazine or newspaper. Neither did I feel any affiliation with left- or right-wing political organizations. I can proudly say I was totally apolitical; I found politics, politicians and people who devote their lives to politics devoid of any meaning whatsoever.'

Despite his disinterest in politics, Akdoğan was thoroughly aware of the inequalities inherent in Turkey's social fabric. He lived with his family in a *site*, those housing developments inside the city protected by private security guards and cut off from the rest of the world. They had four television sets in their apartment. Even when he discovered that his world was tiny and isolated from outside, the observations he made about economic and social inequalities there did not lead him into politics.

When he was 17, Akdoğan wrote a book entitled *I Am Always 17*. In it he explored different aspects of being a teenager, focusing mostly on love and sexuality. He was explicit in his approach to his subject material; almost all the chapters of his book were built on erotic tensions. This 142-page book written by such a young person surprised many; it was even more surprising to see the book go into its fourth impression.

Seventeen was an important age for Akdoğan, who devoted his book to Erdal Eren, a key figure for left-wing youth movements in Turkey. Born in the Black Sea city of Giresun in 1961, Eren belonged to a far-left group called Yurtsever Devrimci Gençlik (Nationalist Revolutionary Youth). After the bodyguard of a nationalist politician shot dead a left-wing university student in 1980, Eren had attended protests and, on 2 February that year, killed a young soldier named Zekeriya Önge. Tried in a military court, Eren was given a death sentence. Before his execution, Eren's solicitor argued that his client was younger than 18 and that they could prove it with clinical tests. The court rejected this and Eren was hanged on 13 December 1980.

Thus it was that Eren became the subject of legend for radical youth movements, which represented him as a heroic figure whose age was surreally increased so that the Turkish state could kill him. Today, when a young person dies in Turkey, it is Eren's image and legacy that comes to people's minds.

Akdoğan's interest in Eren began when he came across an article about his execution on the anniversary of his death. Reading the article led Akdoğan to question the circumstances of Eren's death. When Akdoğan saw pictures of him and read the letters Eren had written to his mother while awaiting the decision of his trial, he decided to devote his book to Eren's memory.

After the publication of *I Am Always 17,* right- and left-wing publications approached Akdoğan, and he started making a name for himself as the young star of Turkey's underground literature. An anchor from CNN Turk, who was surprised to see a political icon of his youth being appropriated for readers by a millennial, invited Akdoğan onto his show.

His second book, *She Cried and I Kissed her Tears,* featured on its cover a black and white image of Akdoğan smoking a cigarette. Blurbed by Küçük İskender, Turkey's leading underground poet, the book focused on a 19-year-old's critical look at his society. Running into nine editions it helped Akdoğan make ends meet as an independent young writer. 'It sold well and readers seemed to move away from popular literature for a while', he remembers. 'It felt as if underground literature was popular now and I was famous.' A report in *Akşam* newspaper pointed to a sociological curiosity: 'Turkey's conservatives are growing, as does Turkey's underground literature', its headline read.

With his newfound fame Akdoğan could afford to move away from the privileged world of his parents. 'I have always been more interested in what takes place in back streets. I wanted to focus on the visible beyond the invisible.' With these objectives in mind, he made an important decision: he would move out of his parents' house at the *site*. This was crucial since the *site* life had been playing such a decisive role in making young people of Turkey apolitical, cutting them off from different social classes and forcing them to socialize only with one another. Those known today as 'White Turks' (members of the most privileged sectors of Turkey's society) have partly been a product of this phenomenon. Growing up among socially and economically similar individuals, White Turks have increasingly lived in a bubble of privilege – a situation that resulted in White Turks' alienation from other sectors of society, particularly the urban poor and the working class, which they started viewing in antagonistic terms.

For Akdoğan the crucial step had been to get as far away as possible from his middle-class life. 'I had written my debut book in my bedroom', he tells me. 'Once I started making money from my writing, I moved out of there and never looked back.'

Unlike many young writers whose desperate need to get published forces them to become non-paid followers of elderly figures from the publishing world, Akdoğan worked with a vanity press and, thanks to his skills at self-publicizing, his work found lots of readers and he came to see the book writing business in terms of sales figures.

Akdoğan made other, more literary discoveries during this era: he fell in love with the works of Baudelaire, Rimbaud and

Kafka. He loved their focus on the character of the *flâneur,* a city dweller whose artistic journeys into the heart of modern cities is among the main subjects of modernist writing. 'I started walking three, four hours every day', he tells me. 'I like walking in nature, too, but I prefer walks in the city.' He preferred the conservative neighbourhoods of Tophane and Aksaray over Bağdat Caddesi and Nişantaşı, two heartlands of White Turkey.

Akdoğan started living in Galata in 2011, the year he enrolled at college. Like his parents before him, he loved to move between houses and ended up living in nine different apartments in the course of less than four years. He stayed mostly on the Serdar-ı Ekrem street in Galata where rents are high. Once he ran out of money, he moved to the next neighbourhood. In Tophane he lived with a group of bohemians. 'We were like refugees. There was this 30-year-old painter, a 40-year-old literary critic, a university undergraduate and me.'

Akdoğan spent his freshman year with fellow film students. Together they made experimental films. He describes their mood before Gezi this way: 'We were aware of what was going on in Turkey but did nothing about it. We thought: "hey, maybe we can do something about life through our art."' He describes film students as 'quite closed to the outside world'. Friends made fun of Akdoğan's films, which he accepts are quite amateurish, but says at least those films brought him to the streets to film them.

It was during this time Akdoğan started observing an animosity between the young and the elderly, the outsiders and the locals. Around Galata Tower, tourists would come and make music during the night. Akdoğan found that he had an ambivalent stance about the matter: 'I empathized with young people there who had to deal with the police, but then I found myself empathizing with the locals. They told me stories about young people drinking like mad and throwing up around the tower and peeing and taking a shite there.' One day in 2012, when Akdoğan was drinking a bottle of beer there with his musician friends, policemen arrived to order them to clear the premises immediately. Young people would no longer be allowed to sit in groups around the tower, they learned.

For Akdoğan this was the opening shot of a process that aimed to bring citizens out of the public sphere. The previous year restaurant tables that were placed on the streets were ordered to be removed (the reason was that they prevented pedestrians from walking comfortably on the pavements). 'I have to walk in this city all the time', Akdoğan says. 'There are no benches to sit on. They have left no public spaces to rest or socialize in. Your only option here is to sit at a cafe and spend a fortune on some fancy beverage.'

Despite such problems Akdoğan lived well; he worked in television for a year and joined the writing team of a programme on books. He was paid handsomely; his books sold well; he lived in a beautiful apartment in Bebek, a wealthy neighbourhood by the sea where the founder of comparative literature, Erich Auerbach, lived during his exile from the Nazi regime.

During May Day in 2013, Akdoğan was walking from Bebek to Beşiktaş when the sight of streets covered by clouds of tear gas shocked and appalled him. 'That day I realized how living in Bebek was similar to going to a private college, as I did in my youth. Not that I complained about it. Living in different worlds and seeing different worlds turned out to be good experience for me.' And yet, when he came back to Bebek that day, Akdoğan was disgusted to see people enjoying life as if nothing was happening in a very close neighbourhood.

By the end of May, Akdoğan had already moved to a new apartment, this time in Tophane. Three weeks later he found himself in an interesting situation. 'I was going out with this girl who asked me to go to Gezi Park with her. I did not want to go there at first; but then, in order to win her heart, I said yes.'

On 27 May Akdoğan played his *flâneur* role once again as he entered the park with his new girlfriend. 'I remember being so surprised to see her putting on a gas mask before we stepped in there. She said, "I heard so many bad stories about the park. It can't hurt if we took some precautions."'

Akdoğan and his girlfriend were in the park when cops burned the tents. He describes how he spent days there without sleep. 'We would come back to Tophane to take a shower before returning to the park.' Meanwhile their neighbours in Tophane became suspicious as they watched them entering and leaving the apartment in their activist outfits (backpack, trainers and a scarf).

In the park, Akdoğan quickly made a discovery: after seeing all the flags and banners of radical parties there, he realized how the only flag he was happy to march under belonged to the LGBTI movement. 'The flag is the biggest totalitarian symbol', he muses. 'When you have a flag, you are automatically dictating something. As an existentialist, I accept none of those. My only exception to this rule is the rainbow flag because I find it so colourful.'

While in Gezi, Akdoğan made a second discovery. The only thing that gave him pleasure in life was to walk through different groups and become a man of crowds. 'The pleasure lay in experiencing the atmosphere there', he says.

The next day, when riot cops started attacking protestors, Akdoğan's world started changing. This was the first time he witnessed police violence. 'If there was one thing that could change me, this was it', he remembers thinking. 'When I witnessed police violence there first hand, I started thinking about what had been going on in eastern Turkey. Witnessing at first hand how the uprising was misrepresented in the media, I decided this must have been the case in the southeast for many decades.'

Wearing a small white-painted mask, Akdoğan went to the park every day, where he gathered ideas for his new novel *Duvar* (The Wall). 'It is about this young guy who undergoes a process of transformation in the course of a set of protests,' he explains, 'and about this girl who changes him.'

Besides providing good material for his book, the Gezi events had transformed Akdoğan's mindset. 'Gezi was not a political protest,' he muses, 'it was an existentialist event ... Some people there demanded change in the political system, and asked for the removal of borders and other things. I wanted those, too, of course. But then I thought, *I* was changing as those events took place, and this change in my character was even more important than a change in the political system. It was one of those once-in-a-century things and the events transformed the young generation.'

Akdoğan was delighted to see people lying on the grass and reading books in Gezi. He was one of those figures lying in the park with a book at hand and a grin on his face. 'The most beautiful thing about the uprising was the library they had built there. There were books by my favourite poets, Ece Ayhan and Turgut Uyar.' He also points to how readers of his beloved Turkish novelists, Oğuz Atay and Sabahattin Ali, increased after the events.

Events affected the literary style of his books. 'For six years I had employed first person singular narrators in my books.

After Gezi I raised my head and realized that I was not alone. There were so many others who were like me. So I wrote their story using the third person singular. This was how my transformation began.'

In this new book Akdoğan focused on LGBTI people, beggars, immigrants, all the people he thought were made others in Turkish society. He made use of the little notes he took during Gezi. It took him a year and a half to transform his impressions and experiences into a novel. 'I did not want to do it hastily', he says. 'If I am doing underground literature then I can't write about something just because it is fashionable. There were many books after Gezi but they all seemed like Gezi-porn to me.'

While writing his novel Akdoğan knew that his audience would not consist solely of protestors. 'I talked with young cops in Gezi; there was this 22-year-old riot cop who recognized me. "Hey brother, I know your work," he told me, "I like underground literature, too." He was lying on the grass, with his gun beside him. My friends were outraged to see me chat with him and were like, "Aytuğ, what on earth were you thinking? Come here!"' This episode reminded Akdoğan of the Italian film director and theorist Pier Paolo Pasolini, who once said he had sympathy for cops during student protests in Italy, since most of them came from working-class families, as opposed to more bourgeois young protestors.

A year and a half after his arrest Akdoğan was cleared of charges against him. Paradoxically it was capitalism that saved him: a credit card slip from a hamburger restaurant proved he was in Taksim during the time he was accused of attacking cops in Kadıköy. He finds it funny that records of his financial transactions were taken seriously, while his statements were not.

'After my ordeal I started to love life more', he tells me. 'Before my arrest I was very pessimistic and I had this inexplicable sadness in my soul. With the court case I had a very concrete reason to worry; I spent those 18 months saying to myself, "Why not go to a concert tonight, maybe I will end up in a prison cell and will no longer listen to music ..." Or, I was like, "let's visit this town that I have always wanted to visit, or else I will have to dream about it in my prison cell."'

The night before the decision was made for his release, Akdoğan was in an extremely anxious mood. He was notified about the final hearing hours before and he spent the night with his lover. 'I hugged her, praying to be released the following day.'

In Kartal the next day the judge asked for his final statement and Akdoğan repeated his desire to be released. Before freeing him from charges brought against him, the judge made a reference to 'every Turkish citizen's legal right to attend public gatherings'. Although he did not attend one on that September day, Akdoğan apparently had the right to attend a protest march if he chose.

'Outside court we took a selfie with my best friend who came to all the hearings with me. Then I went to the beautiful neighbourhood of Moda, and together we rode a seesaw and watched girls passing by.'

This was a moment of victory, but perhaps a pyrrhic one. Over the last year, thanks to anxieties that came along with his court case, Akdoğan found it increasingly difficult to make ends meet. Although Turkish editions of fashion magazines like *Vogue* and *Marie Claire* have featured his portraits in their pages, he is no longer able to make a living from his writing. Poignantly, Akdoğan has returned to the *site*, and is once again living with his parents.

I met Lara Fresko in an Istanbul cafe called Şimdi, which means 'Now' and is pretty close to SALT Beyoğlu, the city's arguably most exciting contemporary art institution which has strong connections to Fresko's past.

A few months before the uprising began in Istanbul, Fresko was among those who conducted research for a show at SALT called 'Scared of Murals' which ended almost exactly a month before events in Gezi began. Documenting the position of Turkish artists during the period 1976–80, the exhibition's aim was to 'investigate what can be excavated and reinvigorated in the hope of presenting possibilities that exist outside of the hegemonic marketization of the art world that marks our current time'. At the time curators described the subject of their exhibition this way: 'The intellectual left, comprised of musicians, actors, writers, directors and photographers, played an active role in the shaping of the political culture from the 1960s until the mid-1970s. However, as political and mass movements took centre stage, in the second half of the same decade, intellectuals lost their primacy.'

In preparation for the exhibition, Fresko and a group of young art historians spent almost a year studying the history of Turkish political art. Together they conducted research at the press archives of DISK (Confederation of Progressive Trade Unions of Turkey) and were surprised by the large number of Turkish artists working with revolutionary groups and organization committees to produce banners, posters and other artistic works in support of Turkey's revolutionary movements in the 1970s. Fresko was shocked to see how profoundly Turkey's leftist groups had been fragmented during the 1970s; she and her co-researchers struggled to map out a genealogy and collected a rapidly growing mini-archive of newspaper clippings on Turkish political art. 'Scared of Murals' pointed out complex interactions between artists and revolutionaries from 1975 onward, its title perfectly summing up the position of authorities in relation to political art. Like Turkish politicians in the 2010s, those once-mighty figures were terrified to see the city politically and artistically transformed into something they were unable to control.

Fresko, a dark, curly-haired and self-confident curator-cum-art-historian-cum-political-theory-enthusiast, had little desire to glorify this history in the show. 'I was talking to fellow researchers and curators and I was like, "hey, we are not romanticizing the history of Turkey's left, okay?" I was this dictator who told everyone the same thing!'

But when, four weeks after the closing of the exhibition, a similar convergence of artists and revolutionaries appeared on the horizon, Fresko allowed herself to be a bit more emotional. Full of excitement, she texted a colleague at SALT and asked: 'Maybe we had a hand in this?'

She couldn't resist the thought. For months tens of thousands of people saw advertisements for 'Scared of Murals' on streets, metro stations and newspapers, and although it would be absurd to even attempt to explain the uprising with one art show, Fresko enjoyed the idea of drawing a parallel between art and life.

'I know it is a naive thought, but we may well have contributed to the zeitgeist leading to the events', she tells me while drinking water from a small glass, before adding that they were also influenced by the zeitgeist in coming up with the exhibition in the first place. 'I had taken pictures of all the banners, flags and artistic material hung on the facade of the

Atatürk Cultural Centre during the uprising. It is a nice feeling to see a connection between our show and such a sublime event.'

Fresko comes from an Istanbul family who, according to her description, raised their only child as a 'million dollar baby'. A single child, she studied at private schools from the start.

Fresko's parents had both spent their youth abroad: her mother went to college in Paris while her father studied at the University of Bath. Fresko is a big fan of her father. 'He is a left-democrat to his very core!' she says, defining her father as 'not a *liberal* democrat but a *left* democrat person ... Our political positions could not have overlapped more.'

Fresko's father got his leftist formation partly from England, where he had spent his university years reading Penguin Modern Classics. 'He confesses to having little time for studying engineering', she says. After finishing his studies in 1976 he had returned to Istanbul where, in 1982, he met his future wife. Fresko was born four years later.

At the age of 14, Fresko was forced to make a shocking discovery, one that concerned the gruesome realities of the Holocaust. One day their neighbour's son pushed her into a corner and shouted in her ear: 'Do you know what people like you become? Soap! That's what you should end up as ... soap!'

After this first encounter with anti-Semitism, Fresko rushed to her apartment and started crying. 'My mother was beside herself with anger', she recalls. 'The bubble they had created around me had burst with that boy's attack on that day.' Her parents had always struggled to keep Fresko away from the horror but here it was, manifesting itself through this racism. 'After that I was constantly aware of being a minority in this society', she recalls. She also got accustomed to hearing people ask a question she would encounter, again and again, for the rest of her life: 'Lara Fresko? What kind of a name is that?' 'These absurd things happen in Turkey all the time', Fresko tells me. 'I think there is more discrimination against minorities among the most privileged sections of society. Those more privileged Turks who feel entitled to all the privileges the country has given to them, think they have the right to question you. They are the normal ones whereas you are seen as abnormal. Had I studied at a public school with less privilege around me I might have faced less discrimination.' Fresko was a very social, albeit 'dissonant' teenager who failed to integrate with kids around her. 'I was the underdog', she says. 'At high school all my friends were neoliberals! They all read Kant! Most of my friends were, or in time became, liberals and neoliberals. There were no leftists around. But nationalists were there in plenty. They would say things against headscarved women, arguing against their right to enter universities ... I thought that they were just parroting received ideas, as was I, for some considerable time.'

When the Turkish parliament started debating a law that would give equal rights to graduates of Imam Hatip schools (secondary education institutions that trained government-employed imams) and private school pupils, Fresko was concerned. Many believed that schools attended by under-privileged pupils did not offer the same educational standards as those attended by 'White Turks', so the pupils of the former had to work much harder in order to compete with pupils from private schools, who enjoyed a higher 'factor' used to calculate grades during university exams.

'I was like, how on earth can we compete with them? After a while, I understood how selfish my feeling was', Fresko says. 'Many people never admitted that the whole thing was grossly unfair. I realized it much sooner.'

Fresko realized other things, too: she witnessed the secular government banning headscarved girls from entering universities. 'My best friend at college came from a conservative family', she remembers. 'She is one of the five brightest people I know on this earth. She did not wear the headscarf but her family was quite conservative. The possibility that this genius of a person would not be admitted to a private university if her parents or she decided that she should cover her hair – not that they did – was incomprehensible for me. I thought, "there is no way this could be fair!" That was the biggest rupture in my life.'

Another rupture came in 2007, during the Republican Protests. There Fresko encountered two types of reaction to the marches against the ruling conservative party. There were those who were over the moon about the protests which they supported wholeheartedly. Then there were others who mocked it with similar passion.

'I belonged to the latter group,' Fresko laughs, 'the group that just couldn't understand what all the fuss was about. What Turkey experienced at that time was a transfer of capital from one group of business people to another. I could see it back then. The central message of the marches was so absurd. I laughed at all those wealthy people carrying Turkish flags and marching in front of Akmerkez [one of Turkey's most luxurious shopping malls] ... I was like, "hey, is this a joke? You think you will be able to fool anyone with this rhetoric?" Those protestors acted as if everything was taken away from them. This was the source of their outrage. At the time I was reading books by Rıfat Bali, a historian of the Turkification of Turkish economy in the early twentieth century. He shows how that was achieved by the confiscation of minority properties that belonged to Jews and Armenians, to create this privileged class. When rich Turks started complaining that things were stolen from them, I found it incredible that they could talk about stealing things, considering their history.'

Encounters with high school friends showed Fresko how many people expected her to be somehow indebted to the Turkish state. 'One of them asked whose side I would be on, if there was a war between Israel and Turkey. I was like, "I will be on the side of Switzerland! Why ask such silly questions?" And they were like, "but you are indebted to this country Lara ... You owe many things to Turkey ..." Now, I never went to a public school, was not even once treated at a public hospital. So I did not owe one penny to this country.' Looking at her diaries before the day of our meeting, Fresko remembered how she was mocked by friends when she told them that if she had a child she would like to raise her in a place with lots of good museums. Fresko enrolled at the private Sabancı University where she took classes on art, art theory and political philosophy. For her graduate studies she decided to focus on arts and their relationship to politics. In 2009, when she was 23, Fresko got her first job: she started working at a contemporary art gallery named Rodeo. For the first time in life she moved outside her ordinary daily route. She tells me about how she used to take the bus from the seaside neighbourhood of Ortaköy, where she lived with her parents, to Tophane, a conservative neighbourhood where support for the ruling party is high.

One day in 2009, Fresko's grandmother, who had moved to London in 1976, called her to ask how her grandchild was

doing. 'I told her I would call her back after I got off the bus',
Fresko remembers. 'A bus? Why are you on a bus?' her grandmother asked. 'I told her I needed to take the bus to get to
this gallery where I worked. "A gallery? Where is the gallery?"
came the answer. When I told her it was in Tophane, my
granny was like, "Tophane! Why should you have anything to
do with Tophane?"'

When Fresko's grandmother left Turkey, Tophane had
a reputation for being a dangerous neighbourhood. Public
transport in Istanbul, too, was considered risky. During the
1990s, public commuting in Istanbul was a hellish experience
for many; Fresko did her best to stay away from buses. At the
time, only the wealthy could enjoy the privilege of commuting
comfortably in the city with their private vehicles. Lower
middle classes and the urban poor, meanwhile, could only
afford buses; rich parents advised their children against using
those vehicles so as to protect them from contact with 'others'.
After the opening of Istanbul's metro line in the noughties,
this state of affairs changed. 'Public commuting was no longer
a nightmare', Fresko says.

Thanks to her new job at the Tophane gallery, Fresko made
another contact and came to know the conservatives, with
whom she would have quite a complex relationship.

On 5 October 2009, Fresko was working at Rodeo gallery
when she heard some worrying noises outside. During the
day the International Monetary Fund and World Bank had
held their annual meetings in the heart of Istanbul, where they
were met with thousands of protestors. This was how *Today's
Zaman* reported the clashes:

Police fired tear gas and used water cannon to disperse the protesters.

Riot police armed with shields and firing gas canisters rushed to disperse protesters in Taksim square, only a few hundred metres (yards) from the IMF–World Bank meetings.

'Long live freedom. IMF get out of our city', protesters chanted.

Police detained around 100 people, some for throwing petrol bombs near the convention centre where finance ministers, central bankers and economists have been meeting to discuss the global economy, broadcaster CNN Türk reported.

The main square and surrounding streets were largely returned to calm by midday, although police were still pursuing small groups of protesters, who appeared to be largely Turkish, in side streets.

The protests were organized by several Turkish unions.

Protesters huddled in hotel and shop entrances rubbing their eyes affected by tear gas fired into the crowd by riot police. Some covered their faces with red scarves. The main pedestrian İstiklal street was briefly deserted as people fled the clashes.

The front windows of several banks were smashed. Police later led out of one branch staff and customers who had been hiding on the first floor of the building. The screens of cash machines at several banks were also smashed.

One student was temporarily detained last week after throwing his shoe at IMF Managing Director Dominique Strauss-Kahn during a speech at the Bilgi University. The shoe missed its target.

There is significant opposition among Turkish students to the IMF, which helped bail Turkey out of a deep financial crisis in 2001. Turkey and the IMF are negotiating a possible new loan agreement after the last one expired more than a year ago.

Fresko watched from inside the gallery how the police intervened against the protestors and was shocked at what she witnessed. 'Protestors started escaping from Istiklal Avenue and came to Tophane. I saw cops with guns running after them. Then shopkeepers materialized on the street and caught the protestors, beating them hard before handing them to cops, who would beat the protestors a second time ... And there I was, watching all this behind the window of the gallery. It was shocking to see our neighbours being capable of doing such things.'

This was followed by another shock that hit even closer to home. On 22 September 2010, art galleries in Tophane came under attack from locals. This was how *Hurriyet Daily News* reported the events:

On Tuesday night, a group of dozens of people, largely young men, attacked an opening event at several art galleries in the Tophane neighbourhood, part of Istanbul's Beyoğlu district. The attackers put at least five people in the hospital with injuries from pepper spray, broken bottles, batons and knives. Seven people were detained, one Tuesday night and six during the day Wednesday, in connection with the incident, but all were released Wednesday night because they could not be identified.

Police came to the galleries Thursday to ask for

security camera recordings, but the cameras were not operative in at least one gallery.

Local residents who spoke to the *Hürriyet Daily News & Economic Review* on Thursday all said the incident started with a verbal confrontation between some gallery visitors who were smoking in the street, drinks in hand, and a woman wearing a chador. Some of the visitors allegedly insulted the woman and the local youth reacted, residents said.

Fresko remembers the atmosphere before the attack. 'I was walking from Outlet to NON, two leading galleries in the neighbourhood, when I saw friends who carried beer bottles in their hands. I asked them to hide those bottles, but they said no, thinking I was exaggerating. "Hey, I am not exaggerating, people here don't want to see this stuff", I told them. Those friends, who had never been to Tophane in their lives, did not exactly know the place.'

Afterwards, at an artist hangout called Urban on Istiklal Avenue, Fresko heard people talk about the attack. 'Some folks were like "oh you see how those animals behave when confronted with artists!" I found such talk very disturbing.'

The day after the events Fresko went to Tophane to inquire about what had happened. She came across a shopkeeper and told him how she hadn't expected such behaviour from him. 'Why didn't you protect the guests?' Fresko asked him. 'We would protect *you* if you came here since we know you', he replied. 'I have seen you here before. But who were those guests? I didn't see them before in my life. Why should I protect them?'

According to Fresko, although many people in Tophane trust and support the conservative party, they have little idea about how they will be affected by a new project called

GalataPort, which could cost them their jobs once implemented. The project's website offers the following information about the planned port:

Located at a very crucial point in Istanbul, and having survived many centuries as the gate to the sea, the GalataPort will reclaim various functions with the new project, and will complement an additional value to Istanbul as a centre of culture, tourism and commerce ... GalataPort project covers over 1.2 km zone with an open area of 100,000 m$^2$ and a construction area of 151,665 m$^2$, where the existing buildings will be harmoniously renovated respecting their authentic forms and acquire new functions. As a result, when the project is completed, Galata will be integrated with Beyoğlu, and this very precious part of the Bosphorus will enjoy a brand new aesthetic value and further contribute to Istanbul ... The architectural design takes in to account all the functions that will provide commercial income in the 1.2 km shoreline, which is outside the customs zone. Both the tourists and the natives of Istanbul will be able to benefit from the offered resources on a 24-hours basis throughout the year. An art museum, hotels, restaurants, bars, fast food joints, all kinds of souvenir shops, shopping centres, office spaces, exhibition and fair areas, car parks and various sales points will ensure an accountable return as a result of the project.

'Tophane locals will lose their jobs once GalataPort arrives', Fresko says. 'In the new economic climate of Turkey, anyone can be extracted from anywhere.' She explains Gezi through a similar perspective. 'Protests to preserve the Emek Theatre from destruction, the strike of airline workers at Turkish Airlines and the green movement's activities all contributed to it', she says. 'It was the bubbling up of the cost of Turkey's economic expansion.' This was a point Fresko had stressed in a blog for *frieze* magazine on 28 August 2013. 'It's important to note that, though unexpected, this movement didn't appear out of thin air', she wrote, three months after the uprising began. 'It's the cumulative outburst of many little movements in many aspects and geographies of life. Its roots extend from struggles against urban transformation and displacement to rural grassroots movements against small-scale hydroelectric dams, nuclear plants and other projects that indiscriminately consume and which obliterate our common resources ... The Gezi Park events have grown to embrace all of these deeply rooted issues and movements. Even if it was at some point most directly about urban transformation, the underlying neoliberal policies have connected these movements.'

While watching the storming of the park by the police on her laptop, Fresko felt her heart miss a beat. She stormed out of her apartment in Galata and was among those who helped bring more tents into Gezi. She thought, like many others who had watched the recent experiences in Egypt's Tahrir Square and the Zuccotti Park in New York, that this was a good tactic to occupy the place and secure it against security forces.

It was 10 a.m. when Fresko was getting ready to part with a friend in front of the Divan Hotel adjacent to the park. 'We were saying goodbye: he would go to work and I would go on with my day ... Then I saw riot police approaching us. I had never been subjected to tear gas in my life and this was my first contact with riot cops. I didn't know what was in store for us and I shouted at them: "Hey, this is your park too!"'

This was not received well. Fresko saw one of the armed water cannons which so terrified Gezi protestors materialize a few metres away from her. TOMA ('Intervention Vehicle to Social Events') is 3.6 metres high, 2.5 metres wide and weighs around 5 tons – quite an intimidating presence. Fresko's friend immediately pulled her to his side, but it was too late. TOMA had started spraying Fresko and people around her; she saw tear gas canisters flying from above. 'We started running in the direction of Nişantaşı. I saw three gas canisters flying past me. Someone in the crowd managed to grab one of the canisters and throw it back to the cops. I could not breathe. I was certain I would die there. "Good job, Lara!" I told myself. "So that's how your life is supposed to end."' Then, once she turned the corner, she threw herself on the ground. What followed was a big surprise. Fresko saw three men were holding her. One sprayed water with Talcid chewing tablets on her face which had a healing effect. Another fellow placed a lemon in her hand. 'I don't think I have felt better in my life', she remembers thinking. Through this five-minute-long experience, her biggest fear (for her life) and joy (the solidarity shown to her) were realized.

'I think the common feeling for all of us who went to Gezi was hope rather than anger', Fresko tells me. 'For the last 25 years we had been sitting in our rooms. And it was anger that had kept us there! Suddenly hope entered the scene: we got the feeling that we could change things, that something could happen, that what we did at the park was important. When you are angry, you stay at home and simmer. When I went to the park for the first time, after my heart missed a beat, I realized that despite all the atmosphere of fear produced on social media, despite all our paranoia about what could be going on there in the streets, there was nothing to be afraid of.' The mood in the park was festive and she felt the spirit of solidarity deep in her bones. 'Going to the street had a calming, restive effect on us', she says. 'The mood was like: "Bring it on! We don't care about what happens to us any more!" This for many was a transformative feeling.'

For the duration of ten days Fresko and her friends experienced what they had dreamed about for a long time: an alternative economy where 'capitalist destruction is counterweighted by a whole host of other modalities such as workers' cooperatives, communes, gift economies, voluntary self-aid organizations and the like'.

'Street vendors who came to Gezi to sell their stuff had to go back empty-handed', Fresko remembers. 'People were sending along free food all the time. It was crucial to show people that such an alternative existed. When I went there the first time, I was reading J. K. Gibson-Graham's *A Post-Capitalist Politics* ... It felt as if it could not be more relevant to what we experienced in Istanbul.'

Nevertheless Fresko did her best not to romanticize the uprising. 'There was this very large, hegemonic crowd of nationalists there as well', she says. 'All they did was sing the Turkish national anthem and repeat the motto, "I am a Turk, honest and hardworking ..." There were certainly groups there who expected to witness a military coup. I saw people walking towards Nişantaşı and getting all excited to see military vehicles going out of the military museum. "The soldiers will save us now!" they must have thought, but then those soldiers started attacking them, too. I was like, "Hey, they are not on your side, time to face the facts!"' Such episodes made it harder for her to romanticize what happened in the park.

Meanwhile Fresko received some good news from London: she was accepted on the summer school programme she had applied to at Birkbeck University. In July, weeks after her experiences in the Istanbul protests, she made her way to London where she started studying with Costas Douzinas, professor of human rights at Birkbeck and the author of *Philosophy and Resistance in the Crisis: Greece and the Future of Europe*. He showed their class a video about Greek protestors destroying public advertisements and talked about how such things were misused by mainstream media to produce a hate discourse against protestors. Fresko knew exactly what he meant.

Another professor Fresko studied with that summer was the French philosopher Etienne Balibar. 'Balibar gave a lecture about his reading of the works of Louis Althusser and Althusser's concept of "the encounter". Hearing him, I couldn't help but think of Gezi where we had just the kind of encounter described by Althusser – an answer to the call of politicization.'

Fresko returned to Istanbul in autumn 2013 and was disappointed by that year's Istanbul Biennial which was held in September, while the protests were still continuing on the streets. The Biennial focused on the notion of the public domain but refrained from featuring artworks that were actually placed in the public sphere. 'The Biennial attempted to impose control on Gezi events and this created a reaction among the artistic community', Fresko says.

'During the uprising, artists had produced numerous subtle, sublime works. They painted a crane pink; there were other interventions to the public sphere. The Biennial had an impulse to appropriate this but they didn't get what had happened there at all. Protestors in the park had done their art anonymously, rather than as individuals. A new ethics had glimmered there which told people to appropriate things to the "commune" instead of institutions and individuals ...'

And this was something artists had done in the Turkey of the 1970s, the subject of 'Scared of Murals'. Before leaving Şimdi, which happens to be located in a very graffiti-rich neighbourhood, Fresko tells me how that show had attempted to carry the knowledge of the previous generation to modern youth. 'Young people in Turkey are forced to discover America again and again', she muses. 'For protest movements to succeed, people need to learn from the experiences of others, of those young people who came before them. This is, after all, part of what art does: it creates access to previous eras and produces new forms of encounter between those living then and now.'

As hundreds of heavily armed riot cops attacked young protestors who objected to the building of an Ottoman era-style building at Gezi Park, film maker Can Evrenol was preparing to shoot a film about a police raid on a derelict Ottoman building inhabited by a satanic cult.

'A horror film featuring the Turkish police was something unprecedented in Turkish cinema', Evrenol remembers as we sit in a street cafe in Moda, on the Anatolian side of Istanbul, where he lives with his fiancée (now wife), a fashion designer. 'And then Gezi happened!' he says and suddenly gets up from his chair, having seen a friend passing by. During our two-hour interview numerous other young people come to our table, a sign of Evrenol's popularity in the neighbourhood.

'I had to postpone the shooting of the film, you see. After the events began our production team started going to the park and stayed in tents.' Evrenol's first idea was to make a documentary of the whole thing. Indeed, he shot hours of footage before handing the project to a friend who works for VICE ('you should be the Michael Moore of this uprising!' was his pitch to the reporter, who later quit the project for personal reasons). Meanwhile Evrenol focused his energies on helping activist friends.

One day during the uprising, at around four in the morning, Evrenol's phone rang. His girlfriend could barely speak. She was hiding in the German Hospital in Taksim, having found herself there after being caught in clashes between protestors and cops. 'Somehow the cops had managed to break into the hospital and the protestors took refuge in different clinics and departments', Evrenol says. 'She was hiding in the radiology department.' What happened next was eerily similar to the kind of violent films Evrenol loves to watch and make.

'I arrived at Taksim in a cab with a friend. Although dusk had fallen it was impossible to see a thing. A thick mist of tear gas hung on the air. It was incredibly scary: there was nobody around and I thought that the moment I stepped onto the street, the cops would materialize from all corners. It was very difficult to get near the hospital where the tear gas was at its densest.' They slowly and carefully approached the building, where Evrenol was able to save his girlfriend in a very cinematic fashion before returning home.

The following day, during another confrontation with the riot police, Evrenol and his girlfriend found themselves in Nişantaşı, Istanbul's Mayfair-like neighbourhood where only the most luxurious brands can afford to open shops. Again,

Evrenol considered this a very film-like setting. 'There were all these incredible-looking young activist girls ... They had tattoos and dreadlocks. I could see they were super-cool and artsy types. When the cops started gassing them those girls pointed their green lasers in the cops' faces to block their view. It was totally like that music video Romain Gavras had shot for Jay Z and Kanye West's "No Church in the Wild".' Gavras's music video depicts around two hundred rioters and police fighting each other in the Czech Republic; there are aesthetically captivating scenes of young protestors being choked by police, cops being set on fire, while green lasers are used to point to divisions between the two sides.

'Girls were carrying red torches and the whole scene was covered in smoke', Evrenol remembers, taking pleasure in his description of the scene. 'In front of the Louis Vuitton shop, police started throwing gas bombs. There could not be a more cinematographic scene ... Just put it into your film and it would work like a dream!'

The scene would fit perfectly in Evrenol's first feature film *Baskın* ('The Raid'), the script of which he wrote shortly before the Gezi uprising. Initially shot as a short, it became feature length once Evrenol found funding.

'I used cops as authority figures in my film', Evrenol says, drinking a glass of lemonade. While researching for *Baskın* he was surprised to discover how in classic Turkish cinema, film makers had no other choice but to portray the police force in a positive light. 'Until the 1980s, all superhero films in Turkish cinema end with awkward scenes, with cops rather than superheroes coming to the crime scene and saving the day ... The reason behind this absurdity was a law which said that at the end of a film, laws of the land, represented by the Turkish police, must reign supreme. There was no other way!'

Evrenol wanted to introduce a novelty to the genre by realistically portraying Turkish cops. Indeed, the five main characters in his film talk and look just like ordinary Turkish cops. The film opens in a shady restaurant where Evrenol's protagonists tell each other stories.

In the opening scene an aggressive cop character describes having sex with a transsexual using homophobic language. Another cop suffers a migraine attack while spending time next to the fireplace. The lead character, a young cop with a troubled past, seems like the most normal figure among them. After being dispatched to a nearby road to check for a police unit which has lost contact with HQ, Evrenol's cop characters set out on the road before hitting someone, or something, that suddenly materializes in front of them. The crash throws them off the road and their van flies into a little brook. Afterwards they realize they are quite close to the derelict building they are supposed to visit. The police vehicle of their colleagues sits outside the entrance like a bad omen. Ignoring the signs, they enter the premises.

The fictional building had served as an Ottoman police station before being turned into a stable in modern times (the republican administration frequently gave mundane, lowly roles to former imperial and religious buildings so as to degrade Turkey's Ottoman past). Although it appears to be deserted at first, the basement floor turns out to be inhabited by a secret cult whose members start to take out the cops one by one, in scenes whose aesthetics can best be described as gory.

'In *Baskın* cops speak about having sex with animals and fucking chickens. They swear very realistically. We showed cops as they had never been shown in Turkish films before. That was our motivation.'

Evrenol's experiences during the uprising (he was gassed numerous times and his fellow film crew members were taken into custody) found their way into *Baskın*. The film is, after all, shot from the point of view of cops who approach something they find impossible to comprehend. The cult whose central mind they are trying to penetrate bears an interesting resemblance to how Gezi protestors had been represented by the jingoistic media: those scary figures make up a group of brainwashed and violent youth controlled by supernatural forces.

As Turkey's leading young horror film maker, Evrenol could not come from a more rationalist and positivist family. He was born into a family of architects, and his mother had a pretty communist mindset. Coming from a right-wing family in Izmir, she had spent her youth hanging out with feminists and socialists and had little appetite for the irrational.

Evrenol's father studied at Istanbul's prestigious Robert College, whose alumni include Turkish Nobelist Orhan Pamuk. 'My father came from this quite Kemalist family', Evrenol says. 'His parents were friends with İsmet İnönü, the second president of the republic. My father used to wear long, charismatic coats and grew his hair while in high school. He went to Germany for his college education and got his German discipline from there. His family was also quite strict and my father was totally into discipline when he came back to Turkey.' Evrenol describes his father's mindset as a curious mixture of German discipline and American conservatism. (Evrenol also has a brother; born in 1986, his younger brother has worked for Microsoft at Seattle and, according to Evrenol, is a more scientifically minded fellow.)

'When I was little our parents would not let us watch TV', Evrenol tells me. 'It had to be turned off during the day. They would make us listen to classical music and look at Renaissance paintings in books.' Their upstairs neighbours were their sole gate to the outside world where Prime Minister Turgut Özal was in the process of constructing a new, liberal economy in Turkey. 'Another neighbour next door would watch soccer games while our television set was firmly turned off. They would listen to arabesque music from their radio while we listened to Turkish jazz musicians like Okay Temiz from our CD player. My parents would say: "Hey, if you don't want to end up like them, you should study a bit harder!"'

Evrenol grew up in Istanbul's Çiftehavuzlar neighbourhood, in an apartment with a large garden. 'I spent my time outdoors, on streets. We really grew up in this *mahalle* [street] culture. Many friends in our generation grew up indoors but I was constantly on the streets. It was so much fun. When I went indoors the atmosphere of discipline would return.'

Evrenol went to a public school where half of the pupils were *kapıcı çocuğu*, sons of apartment doorkeepers. He remembers how he saw no social divisions between himself and his friends with whom he played football until late hours.

'My parents were not snobs but they nevertheless imposed on us a regime of intellectual fascism', Evrenol remembers. 'In secondary school they would drive me to tears just because I watched this television programme called *Televole* about football and gossip.'

Evrenol's father, who passed away in 2014, was a big fan of sci-fi cinema and an inspiration for his elder son. His tombstone is two metres long and has the shape of a monolith which is a reference to his favourite film, Stanley

Kubrick's *2001: A Space Odyssey.* 'My father was an incredibly interesting and open-minded fellow', Evrenol says. 'It was interesting to see how he thought like an American conservative when it came to issues like homosexuality and religion. He was like, "hey, don't say bad things about Allah or he will get sad". When we watched *Philadelphia* together, he was a bit irritated to see Antonio Banderas and Tom Hanks making out in one scene. I remember him saying: "now, of course, these things are a bit contrary to our values ..."'

When he was in high school Evrenol's parents started working for Sinpaş, a construction company whose owners are known to have conservative political views. In the polarized atmosphere of the 1990s, newspapers would frequently publish lists of companies which needed to be boycotted because of their purportedly dangerous political views (conservatism for secularists, Kurdish movement for nationalists, 'Jewish-capital' for religious extremists, etc.).

'My parents had to do lots of soul-searching before accepting the offer', Evrenol remembers. 'Once my parents got the job they realized how much those people respected them. They were proud of my parents, seeing them as "the international face of Turkish architects who now work for our company".' Thanks to their commissions the Evrenol family's yearly income increased greatly; Evrenol tells me how the funding for his latest film, *Baskın,* came from his mother and how 'she got that money thanks to those commissions!'

Evrenol was enrolled at Üsküdar American High School where his closest friends had almost no common interests with him. 'I was one of the popular guys', he remembers and confesses to having participated in some bullying there. 'I bullied some people and was bullied, too. There were those *Lord of the Flies*-like scenes but nothing too serious.'

Politics was out of bounds, thanks to the strict discipline imposed by the school administration. 'I couldn't believe friends from other schools who told me about how they could smoke joints at school ... We had strict discipline: I would be in big trouble if I was not behind my desk with my uniform in perfect order when the school bell rang. I kind of liked that. When they loosened the rules I was disappointed.'

Although a fan of discipline, Evrenol was one of the naughtiest boys in his private school and would often get kicked out of class because he talked too much. 'I also liked vandalizing things', he tells me with a smile in his eyes. 'It was so great to break stuff at the lavatories. It was a way of getting revenge on school.'

To have fun with his friends Evrenol started a film club where they held weekly screenings. He says he had never owned a camera until he decided on a professional film career. 'I was really into Quentin Tarantino's films and I imagined becoming a film director one day.' When it was time to apply to college, Evrenol chose to study international finance at a private university, where he had a miserable time.

Seeing her son bored with life in Istanbul, Evrenol's mother came to the rescue and offered to send him to the US. But Britain turned out to be a better alternative. He had fallen in love with a girl who was on her way to Kent University for her education; Evrenol joined her and decided to take a look at life there. 'I lived with her for a while in Kent and really loved the place. The place was great for sport and there were lots of parties.'

Another factor that made Evrenol want to go to Kent was the mandatory military service in Turkey. 'I was like, I'd rather be poor in England than suffer doing my service in Turkey. I was lucky enough to be eligible to pay my way out of the military.' Evrenol laughs as he tells me about making fun of friends who served, saying things like, 'oh, so you went to the military, it is so *passé*!'

After three years at Kent University, where he studied film theory and graduated with a thesis on Jason Voorhees, Evrenol set his sights on the New York Film Academy, advertisements for which he saw in *Sight & Sound*. During the film workshop at Universal Studios he decided to adapt his favourite short story *Vidalar* (Screws) by Turkish author Sulhi Dölek. Shot in black and white, the film follows a young man who continually finds screws in his house; *Screws* was selected as one of the best ten films that year in Turkey. Evrenol then shot *Sandık* (The Chest) about a boy who terrorizes his small town. Available for free on Vimeo, the film's violence is refreshing but not palatable for everyone.

A big fan of the latest wave of French horror cinema, Evrenol says the best horror films get their energy from societal events. 'The burning of intellectuals in the Madımak Hotel in 1993 was perfect material for a zombie film', he argues. 'There is outrage on the streets, lots of bad feeling and anxiety ... All that stuff needs to be transformed into the language of cinema.' Evrenol says he enjoys films 'that look right-wing politically but actually feature left-wing stuff' and names Paul Verhoeven as the master of this attitude. 'I just love *RoboCop*. Verhoeven found it difficult to work in the Netherlands where the leftist government found his art problematic and he was forced to flee to the US where he produced these great caricatures of American capitalism. I love his excesses.'

I ask Evrenol about censorship: can he really get away with making such films in Turkey and escape the wrath of censors? His answer is quite surprising. 'The only time my work was censored was in Britain', he says. 'London FrightFest Festival asked directors who had previously showed their films there to shoot a minute-long commercial that instructs viewers to turn off their phones during the screening.' Evrenol's film, *Turn Off Your Bloody Phone*, shows a man getting annoyed by a girl who talks on the phone during the screening and stabbing her in her head. Since it was shown in the week of the Aurora Theater massacre in the US, *Turn Off Your Bloody Phone* created lots of anger. The *Huffington Post* reported:

> Written and directed by Can Evrenol – the filmmaker who won the Most Disturbing Short Film at the 2010 HP Lovecraft Festival in Poland – comes a PSA that could shock even the most ardent horror fan. [...]
>
> 'Turn Off Your Bloody Phone' features an audience member whose plea to a female theater patron to stop texting during the film goes ignored. In retaliation, he proceeds to stab her in the back of the head with a pen, pull out her brains, unzips his pants and proceeds to do terrible, unmentionable things.
>
> It's disgusting, it's shocking, but the message to turn off your phone is pretty clear.
>
> Though the PSA was made for a horror festival, which celebrates general violence, terror and repugnance, it's somewhat surprising that organizers would choose to run such a violent PSA in the wake of the Aurora Theater shooting in July. Though the shooting happened stateside the effect was felt around the world, and many theaters including exhibitors in London increased security following the tragic event.

After the *Independent* also reported the news and people argued how inappropriate it was to make such a film in the wake of the

Aurora Theater shooting, FrightFest finally decided to pull the ad. Evrenol was not pleased. 'I made the film free of charge,' he tells me, 'just to please them. And then they censored it.'

Before he shot *Baskın* Evrenol had made a list of all the things he wanted to learn about cops. Thanks to the intermediacy of a friend he was allowed to visit a police station in Istanbul's European side. The inspector there showed Evrenol and his friend how cops handle guns and climb the stairs and greet each other. He talked about how cops talk in private. He informed them about radio stations they listen to, the nicknames they use. He showed them their bodily postures and provided them with information about things like what officers are supposed to do if they fall into the water ('they first check their guns') as well as the procedures cops follow when they come across individuals who claim to be cops (Evrenol's characters come across a zombie-looking cop in one of the darkest scenes of *Baskın*; cops ask for their IDs).

'The inspector really liked us. And we really liked him', Evrenol says. 'Then, somehow, we started talking about Gezi. "My niece went to the protests", he told us. "If I was your age perhaps I would go visit, too." He said protestors were right in the first three days before the protests "turned into something else" in the following days.'

Evrenol believes there is corruption in the Turkish police force while appreciating individual officers in his personal life. A few weeks before we met in Moda, Evrenol and his girlfriend had invited friends to announce some good news: they were getting married that summer. The house party was open to all their friends in Moda and the couple paid little attention to who came and went. So when two new guests rang the doorbell they quickly opened the door.

'There was something funny about their outlook, they looked a bit too grunge', Evrenol remembers. 'I realized they were here to make trouble. They wanted to get inside the apartment. I told them this was a private party. I realized that one of the guys had a huge knife with him. They instructed me to go downstairs and walk in front of them. I really thought they would kill me there. Once downstairs I told them I would bring money to them if they allowed me to go to my room. They were like, "okay, we will wait for you here, but if you don't come back, we will come to your apartment and attack your guests". I rushed to my house, asked friends what to do.' They decided to call the cops.

Once the police arrived, Evrenol and his friends walked downstairs and watched in joy as the cops 'started beating the hell out of them'. Evrenol says he did nothing to stop the cops. On the contrary, he was quite pleased with what they did and confesses to feeling safe thanks to their intervention. 'The cops were incredibly civil when they talked to us afterwards. We looked at them as our saviours. I wanted to tip them for what they did for us.'

Evrenol has nothing personal against Turkey's cops, whom he attempted to represent realistically in his film. Having made open references to Gezi events in the script of *Baskın*'s feature-length version, Evrenol decided that drawing such parallels would be pretentious and eventually removed them. 'I would love it if *Baskın* was shown in all Turkish police stations', he tells me with a smile on his face before I leave him in front of his apartment.

※

31 May 2013. London. A young artist named Serra Tansel has just heard from her circle of Turkish friends living in Whitechapel and Bethnal Green that something interesting is going on in their country. As the evening progresses, they come across calls to attend a rally in Hyde Park scheduled to take place the following day.

Next morning, as she makes her way to Hyde Park, Tansel discerns a large group of protestors holding dozens of red Turkish flags, that unmistakable symbol of Turkish patriotism. They shout slogans used by protestors in Istanbul ('Everywhere is Gezi, everywhere is resistance!').

When she goes to Trafalgar Square the next day she sees two groups. One group recites with increasing passion the Turkish national anthem: *Korkma sönmez bu şafaklarda yüzen al sancak!* ('Fear not, the red flag that swims in those dawns shall never perish!'). She turns her head in the other direction to see the second group, equally large, whose members are also holding flags. Coloured yellow, green and red, their Kurdistan flags are accompanied by posters of Abdullah Öcalan, leader of the armed Kurdish party the PKK which, during the last three decades, has fought against the Turkish state. The violent struggle between the two had unexpectedly paused three weeks earlier, after Öcalan's message of peace with the Turkish state and reconciliation was read in Diyarbakır.

Tansel watches in shock the disagreement between the two groups. While members of the former sing the Turkish national anthem, the other group starts dancing to the traditional Kurdish *halay*, which involves a group of people forming a circle to dance. She hears verbal abuse between members of the groups; tension is in the air. There are attempts to join the forces of two groups; they turn into one big group but then divide again.

'Not going to that march was not an option', Tansel tells me in a Starbucks in Istanbul's Beşiktaş neighbourhood in August 2015, more than two years after the events. Tansel has just returned from an artist's residency in Athens and is in excellent spirits.

'All my Turkish friends were there in the park. Afterwards I was quite irritated to see how polarized people were and how these two nationalist groups had this animosity between them. I was so annoyed that we ended up going to a pub to drink a pint. I was angry to see people fight against each other in London while all those incredible things were going on in Turkey.'

The first marches in Hyde Park and Trafalgar Square were followed by a series of forum meetings in London. Having previously worked in the Arcola Theatre in Hackney, which was founded by the left-wing Turkish theatre director Mehmet Ergen in 2000, Tansel was happy to learn that weekly forums would be organized inside the theatre premises (a few months earlier Tansel had contributed to an Arcola play adapted from Turkish short story writer Sait Faik). The first time she went there for the forums was a warm summer day; there people congregated in Dalston Curve Garden, a beautiful garden adjacent to the theatre, whose owners were experiencing their own struggle against gentrification in London and allowed those angry young people use their premises for free.

During the very first meeting Tansel voiced her frustration about the problems caused by Turkish and Kurdish flags in the demonstrations. 'I was uncomfortable to see flags bearing the image of Abdullah Öcalan', she told the audience, among whose members there were big supporters of the Kurdish leader. 'I don't know why I have felt that way but I confess to having felt this way.' In return she listened to protestors who had been irritated to see Turkish flags. 'You must explain to me why you felt that way and then maybe I can explain my own irritation', Tansel said. 'We need to fix this. In Turkey people are holding hands and showing solidarity, while here, despite facing no police violence, we are at loggerheads with one another.'

The air of animosity disappeared gradually after young protestors came to know each other. Their first resolution at Arcola was not to bring any flag or political image, be it Turkish or Kurdish, to the next protest march.

They brainstormed about alternative ways of voicing their anger and came up with the idea of painting a placard that read STOP VIOLENCE IN TURKEY and smuggling it into the Arsenal–Galatasaray football game in London's Emirates Stadium on 4 August 2013. Since political placards are banned in British stadiums, Tansel and 40 other people from the forum were kicked out of the Emirates Stadium, but were happy to have made the voice of angry young Turkey heard using the unexpected intermediacy of a football match.

Tansel was born in 1989 in Istanbul. Her father trades in steel while her mother, after years in the textile industry, recently started working as a ceramic artist.

The family had spent the past 20 years changing homes in Istanbul. 'My father is addicted to moving houses', Tansel tells me. They first lived in Caddebostan (not far away from Can Evrenol's house) and then moved to Etiler when she was eight. They rented an apartment in Tarabya before going all the way back to Etiler. 'My father always complains about how small our apartments are. After moving to a new place, he changes his tune: "this place is too small, or too big, or too noisy, or too silent for us!"' When she was 15 there was quite a different reason for moving houses: Tansel's parents got a divorce.

Born in 1959 and 1961 respectively, Tansel's parents had different relationships with politics in their youth: he was interested but never became a member of any group; she had no interest in the subject at all. Growing up during the violent years of the late 1970s, which saw the deaths of dozens of street activists from left- and right-wing political groups every day, they witnessed the closing of all universities and a halt to daily life in the country.

Tansel never liked school in Turkey, having a dislike for some of her teachers throughout her education. She found them to be too restrictive: whenever she wanted to play and have some fun in her pre-university life, she was interrupted. This way Tansel came to hate the competitive atmosphere of the school system which, she thought, turned pupils into race horses, every one of them struggling to get the highest grades and outdo one another.

In high school Turkish pupils around Tansel started making 'career plans': most of them wanted to leave Istanbul and go to the US; the most popular pattern for the kids of well-off Turks was to go abroad for half a decade before taking over the reins of their parents' companies upon their return to Turkey. Tansel was an exception to this; she had no desire to continue her father's job, and she was just beginning to show an interest in fashion design. She enrolled at an atelier to study drawing.

One day during her last year at high school, representatives from London's Central Saint Martins came for a visit to the atelier. They were on the lookout for prospective students. Tansel was interviewed and offered a place in the vocational school; she remembers the whole thing as being much easier than she had anticipated. 'The representative looked at my collages. She asked me questions about Istanbul and my life. She said I could choose whether I wanted to study fashion design or art after finishing my first year. A few years later I realized how the higher enrolment fees demanded from Turkish students played a part in the simplicity of the process.'

For Tansel, London seemed like a good place to spend her late teens and early twenties. 'I couldn't comprehend America', she tells me. 'It seemed so different from Turkey and so alien to my character ... I could more easily imagine myself in London.' She had a close friend living in the city and she was happy to be enrolled at a college that didn't require her to take the mandatory central exam ÖSS that all pupils in Turkey take in order to get a place in Turkish universities.

As she was getting ready to leave Turkey, Tansel started having worries about whether she would ever return to her country. 'I could feel how my freedoms were being stifled in Istanbul', she says. When I ask her to be more specific, she says: 'People would give me those weird looks when I wore shorts or acted confidently as a female.' According to Tansel, the polarization in Turkish society had already begun when she got on the plane to Heathrow. 'For me the problem was not what would happen if I stayed in Turkey but whether I would be able to return to Turkey afterwards', she says.

During the three years she spent in London, Tansel made her way into the vibrant artistic atmosphere and met like-minded artists from Turkey. In Bethnal Green and Whitechapel, she befriended figures from Turkey's contemporary arts scene and became neighbours with Turkish artists İsmail Saray and Bora Akıncıtürk.

At Central Saint Martins she was happy to discover that her instructors were open-minded. 'I was happy to see how nobody expected me to produce "Turkish art" or works that needed to explore Turkey', she says. 'They approached all students in the same way. I encountered the orientalist expectation from artists to produce "local" works in the art market in the following years, but it was not there in academia.'

One of the first discoveries Tansel made in London concerned headscarves. 'I used to go to London markets and see all those headscarved women around me', she says. 'Secular Londoners did not give them those bad looks as some Turks did in Istanbul.' She found less conflicts on the surface level; this was the first time Tansel witnessed a harmonious society which, she says, has become more Turkey-like in 2015, after the rise of Islamophobia in Europe.

Another discovery Tansel made concerned the status of immigrants. Now that she was treated like one, she could better understand the plight of immigrants in Turkey and abroad. 'My mother's cleaning lady is a Bulgarian woman named Pembe; she would regularly travel to her homeland to get a stamp on her passport which she needed to legally stay in Turkey. Now, as a Turkish student trying to get a work permit in London after my graduation from college, I could finally empathize with her status.'

Not long ago Felipe Castelblanco, a multidisciplinary artist, initiated a 'ParaSite School' during his fellowship at the Royal Academy School in London. Castelblanco's project aimed to provide 'alternative opportunities for minorities, undocumented migrants and artists facing immigration issues to attend college and access higher education in the US and Europe' and served as a platform for artists like Tansel. During crit sessions organized at ParaSite, Tansel discerned fundamental epistemological differences between herself and European artists. She was not acquainted with biblical Christian imagery as they were; shapes, figures and gestures that could effortlessly be identified as biblical references by others were lost on her.

Tansel's artistic productivity was recognized in London's artistic world: her project *Chance Symphony* was exhibited at Tate Britain, in the museum's Turner room. 'In 2012 I had visited numerous museums alongside my dear Turkish friend Defne who, once we got into a hall, had a habit of saying: "Let's walk here as if we were *buyers*!" and walking in the gallery with heavy steps.' This, for Tansel, provided a hilarious insight into how people were expected to behave in museums: silently, without making any noise. 'I wanted to create a device that would allow visitors to make noises in the museum', she remembers. So she created metal clogs and other wearable instruments visitors could use as footwear. Her *Chance Symphony* managed to turn the visitor into a participant in the artwork.

The year after her graduation from Central Saint Martins, Tansel decided she wanted to work with Martin Creed, the winner of the Turner Prize in 2001 for his *Work No. 227* (the installation featured a gallery with bare walls where the lights go on and off – it was later acquired by Tate Britain). With this idea in mind she went to a talk by Creed; after the end of the talk she approached him and voiced her desire to work with him. Shortly afterwards she became his assistant and, in her words, 'started doing all kinds of work for him, from his accounts to helping him produce his works, to assisting him in the creation of new works, to walking his dog and cleaning his dishes'. This went on for two-and-a-half years and after she quit the job, a new job opening at the Serpentine Gallery – where

Tansel was getting ready to work for Marina Abramovic's *512 Hours* performance – came to nothing because of her status as an immigrant-cum-student.

Back in her studio flat, Tansel decided to organize a show in her hometown. In 2010 the attack against Tophane galleries had upset her and now it seemed like the right time to exhibit a show there that would express her frustration; she wanted to use water as a common ground that could bring together Tophane people while highlighting the issue of water politics. In September 2014 she teamed up with Duval Timothy, her friend from Central Saint Martins, for an exhibition they named *Su İkramımızdır* ('On the House'). Their idea was to use the Polistar gallery in Tophane as a hub from where they could distribute water to visitors.

'I had been thinking about the conflict in Tophane between newcomers and locals from a distance', Tansel says. 'When we went there with Duval, the important thing was to realize that the locals had been living there for a very long time. Locals start feeling like outsiders in their own territory, when these very modern art spaces and cafes which they can't afford to go to, open in their neighbourhood. Their fears, of course, by no means justify the violence of the attackers who wounded people there. But still, Duval and I felt that fragmentation among people there had been a very dangerous thing ... So we developed this project intended to find a common ground between everyone in Tophane.'

Creating an atmosphere in Tophane where people could talk to each other and drink water, one of the fundamental elements of the earth, proved a successful idea. 'The tailor on the street came to visit and so did the car park attendant. There were young artists, street sellers, drivers, shoemakers – all kinds of people.'

Tansel and Duval served water in little ceramic cups they had produced together and were excited to see people from all walks of life go inside the gallery space and be a part of the atmosphere. Tansel, her aunt and a car park attendant chatted for an hour; her aunt later told Tansel: 'I can't believe how wise that chap is!' A *darbuka* player, the 11-year-old street kid Sercan, was invited to the opening; Tansel was happy to see those figures she always came across on Istanbul's different streets come to her show.

'Having this experience really changed my connection with Istanbul', Tansel tells me as we leave Starbucks. Outside in Beşiktaş we find ourselves exposed to the intense heat of the midday sun. Water is what we need right now, I tell myself, and remember how Tansel has used water so interestingly in her art exhibition as the symbol of a unifying force for Turkey's polarized society. This may be one of the best solutions to be offered by angry young Turkey to their country's century-long problems: a glass of water, beautiful and artful in its simplicity.

Young artists, film makers, novelists and poets in Turkey are luckier than their ancestors, who rarely escaped the wrath of the Turkish state. The problems that await today's young artists are more private in nature. They concern their fragile positions in society. Nowadays it is difficult to come across an artist who does not have passionate criticisms about the state of affairs in Turkey; many voice either sympathy or their open support for protestors. And yet, artists rarely define themselves as activists or members of this or that political party in the same way the previous generation of prosecuted artists did.

To me this looks like a triumph for Turkish artists' intellectual independence – they are no master's voice. Just look at the older generation of dissidents, even to such figures as the poet Nazım Hikmet. The artistic careers of these old-school dissidents were defined by their devotion to all-encompassing ideologies, to communism in particular. Hikmet lived in Moscow and devoted most of his late poems to the cause of communism, leaving many readers saddened by his defence of Stalin. Hikmet viewed Turkey in antagonistic terms; as a NATO country, it was a mere puppet of US imperialism in his eyes.

Turkey's most famous film maker in the twentieth century, Yılmaz Güney, had a similar fate: like Hikmet, he was equally admired and feared, loved and despised in Turkey. Imprisoned in numerous Turkish prisons over many years, he had to eventually flee his country, and lived his last years in Paris where he died aged 47. Güney directed his Palme d'Or-winning masterpiece *Yol* (The Road) from afar, with a local crew shooting scenes in Turkey and sending them to France.

My own generation's artists are having problems of a different nature. As a novelist myself I rarely feel the desire to flee Istanbul, a city that stands at the centre of the world's attention. It is dangerous here for artists, but the risks are worth taking when you consider how relevant Turkey's culture has become. Artists, film makers and novelists alike are aware and making use of Turkey's experiences in the past century, its transformation from a multi-ethnic empire to a nationalist republic; its wealth of experiences, contradictions and paradoxes provide attractive material for new art projects.

Unlike the angry young artists of the past century, this generation is more reluctant to take sides; instead they are struggling to interpret and come to terms with the transformation of Turkey. Rather than actors participating in the grand game of politics, artists have become observers of events which they are expected to interpret to an international audience. Despite all the risks and dangers, it is an incredibly exciting time to be an artist in Turkey.

By early September 2015, what has been called 'the desert heats' had left Istanbul; the temperatures finally fell below 30 degrees celsius; the humid nights of the previous three months had come to an end. The political atmosphere, by contrast, was just starting to heat up: after the 7 June elections that resulted in an impasse, snap elections were announced for 1 November.

Meanwhile the art season kicked off with the opening of the Istanbul Biennial. Unlike the decisively political tone of the last edition, the new Biennial focused on the theme of 'salt water', inviting the city's art community, who had spent the past two years debating passionately the subject of politics, to ferry rides around Istanbul's Princes' Islands – in what promised to be a more relaxed atmosphere.

The new season brought novelties to Turkey's young artists, too. When I last spoke to her, Serra Tansel was getting ready for her personal show, 'Serra Tansel Unlimited', scheduled to be exhibited at London's noshowspace gallery from November 2015. After spending anxious summer nights having nightmares about prison life, Aytuğ Akdoğan took refuge in Kabak Valley, a mountainous place with fascinating views of the Mediterranean, a favourite summer location for Turkey's youth. Lara Fresko, meanwhile, was far away from Istanbul, in Ithaca, New York City, preparing for the new academic term at Cornell where she was continuing her doctoral studies. A few days after I spoke with Fresko, Can Evrenol told me he was planning his own travels to the New World. In late August, days before his wedding, Evrenol had heard from the Toronto International Film Festival to say that *Baskın* would have its world premiere on 11 September 2015. Evrenol said his two dreams had come true that summer, two years after the events in Gezi. First, he was united with the love of his life, whom he struggled to protect during the uprising. Secondly, he was now given the chance to show his energetic, violent horror film to the film community in Canada and the US. The weeks they would spend promoting the film, Evrenol and his wife decided, would be their honeymoon.

# CHAPTER THREE

# All the Anger
# That's Fit to Print

The first journalist murdered in Turkey's modern history was not a reformist-minded progressive but a conservative who opposed that group's ideological programme. Hasan Fehmi was the editor-in-chief of Ottoman newspaper *Serbestî* (Freedom) when he was shot dead on 6 April 1909. While walking from Beyoğlu to Sirkeci with his dear friend Şakir Bey, Hasan Fehmi was stopped by a black-moustachioed man who wore a black greatcoat with brightly coloured buttons. 'Al Mevlan!' the guy cried before first shooting Şakir Bey, who survived the attack wounded; he then put three bullets into Hasan Fehmi's body and escaped into the crowd.

The assailant, who was not caught afterwards, had perhaps intended to kill the newspaper's founder Mevlânzade Rıfat, one of the most despised figures of republicans because of his staunch criticisms of the Committee of Union and Progress (CUP).

In Turkey, such episodes are not uncommon. Here words can quickly get an author into trouble if they have not been put into writing cautiously enough.

Both progressives and conservatives enjoy silencing the dissenting voice of the opposite camp; following the assassination of Hasan Fehmi, supporters of the progressive CUP party were chased and attacked on Istanbul's streets, an event that forced dozens of journalists and intellectuals (including the female novelist Halide Edib) to flee the city.

Things were not better in the pre-CUP era either. The Ottoman Sultan Abdul Hamid II had constructed one of the most effective censorship mechanisms known to history; his network of spies would inform the sultan about any prospective plot against his rule. An army of censors inside the government offices would check every sentence of every article printed in all newspapers of the empire on a daily basis. Here journalists knew that doing their job may result in either getting them censored or killed: this is the legacy faced by young journalists, from both progressive and conservative camps.

On 7 April 2013, editor and film critic Berke Göl was marching with his journalist friends on Istanbul's Istiklal Avenue under the banner *'Emek Bizimdir'* ('Emek belongs to us') when a string of events began that ended with his being choked by a police officer and arrested. Göl, a psychology graduate from Turkey's prestigious Bosphorus University, had not experienced police violence first hand before. He had been working as an arts journalist and was sensitive to political issues in Turkey, but had not known the smell of tear gas or felt the power of a water cannon before. That Sunday afternoon, this young journalist's ignorance about such issues would come to a definitive – and disturbing – end.

Emek, the name of Istanbul's oldest film theatre, means 'labour' in Turkish. The theatre had been defended passionately by left-wing activists since 2010 when it closed its doors to the public. 'Emek is Ours, Istanbul is Ours' was the name of a group of activists who had struggled to save the theatre from destruction; the group's members included film directors, students and critics, actors and festival programmers. Support for them in the media was strong, but there was also a considerable number of writers who wanted to see the Emek Theatre demolished. Some columnists said they would resign from their jobs if plans went ahead and the theatre was demolished, while other urged the government to go ahead with their plans.

Emek activists, most of whom would be on the front line during the uprising in Gezi, employed interesting, and effective, tactics. They would suddenly get up from their seats during gala events of film festivals and start shouting the slogan: 'Emek is Ours! Istanbul is Ours!' This would be followed by applause from the audience. But this was not at all enough to stop the construction on Emek. When a company had rented the property from its owners, there was little activists could do to preserve it. Their efforts, which seemed desperate at the beginning, would prove transformative for Turkey.

Göl was one of those angered at reading reports about Emek's planned demolition and reconstruction as part of a multiplex theatre placed inside a new shopping mall on the same location. The intensity of the debate between city administrators and activists had reached a peak during the second week of 2013's International Istanbul Film Festival, an event that brings most of the country's film critics and arts journalists together (Göl served on the festival's FIPRESCI jury). On 7 April, numerous filmgoers who had previously watched the debate from afar joined the protestors as Göl and his journalist, student and activist friends started marching from the tram stop at the entrance of Istiklal Avenue to Yeşilçam Street, which houses the Emek Theatre and was cordoned off that afternoon by riot police.

Upon reaching the entrance of the street, thousands of protestors defied the cops, asking them to clear the entrance and open the street to protestors. Their goal, they said, was to march on Yeşilçam Street, and thus execute their constitutional right.

Fearful of an occupation of the derelict theatre building by thousands of protestors facing them, the riot cops had a different take on the events. The interior minister would later announce the security forces' decision to cordon off the street: it was, he said, the police's responsibility to protect private property. Since the Emek Theatre was rented by a construction company, it was the police's duty to save it from those who wanted to march towards it en masse. A few minutes later, the clash of these two different stances about a publicly owned, privately rented and historically significant building at the heart of Istanbul would result in scenes of chaos.

'Cops sprayed water and people dispersed immediately. Many tried entering side streets', Göl tells me one March day in a coffee house overlooking the cold waves of the Bosphorus in the seaside neighbourhood of Ortaköy.

'Then there was tear gas. As people escaped, cops continued with their advance. The TOMA started spraying water in our direction. Istiklal Avenue was gradually turning into a little lake. It was all deserted but for the cops who struggled to clear the area. I took refuge in a side street. After a few minutes I wanted to see what was happening on Istiklal.'

This gesture of curiosity would prove to be consequential for Göl. As soon as he took a few steps forward, ten riot cops entered the side street and started running towards him. They were wearing gas masks and riot gear; the time was half past six, sharp. One of Turkey's most important film makers,

Erden Kıral, who also attended the protest, had fainted; Costa Gavras, the legendary film director famed for his political films about human rights abuses, was among the protestors, doing his best to avoid the tear gas.

At around 6.35, a cop wearing a gas mask placed his hand around Göl's throat and held him in a choking position. This image would be broadcast on television that evening – Göl facing this officer, with a shocked expression, spoke volumes about the strained relations between the Turkish state and journalists in Turkey, who had long complained about the lack of free air to breathe in their country. Here was literal, and visual, proof of their complaints.

'Everyone escaped when they saw the cops', Göl remembers. 'But I couldn't accept running away. We were doing nothing wrong there, so why was I supposed to escape?' Then they got him. 'Had I taken refuge in a shop, maybe they would just hit me with their batons and continue with their advance and forget about me. But there I was, on the street, with my hands outstretched in two directions in a pose that asked "what did I do wrong?" A high-ranking cop turned to other officers and said "take him". Hearing this they started pushing me around. I was handcuffed and placed into a police van. Just before I was pushed inside, I cried out: "I am from the press, I am a journalist!" But they ignored this.'

While being arrested Göl recognized, a few metres away from him, the seasoned investigative journalist Ahmet Şık, who had been released from prison thirteen months earlier. Having served a year for writing a book called *The Imam's Army* in which he documented police corruption and a cover-up of the murder of Hrant Dink, Şık was back in the field, photographing the protest (he was wounded that evening while doing his job) and sharing his work via social media. A living

Turkish champion of free speech, Şık's appearance at that difficult moment was important for Göl. 'Brother Ahmet!' he shouted at him. 'They are taking me away! My name is Berke Göl!'

But even this icon of journalism could not save his young colleague. The film critic was driven outside Taksim in a van that shuttled between different locations to pick up different activists arrested that day. One of those detained had fainted because of the tear gas, while Göl was physically okay but also awestruck by what had happened to him.

After the medical checks, Göl was brought to Vatan Street where, following the public prosecutor's orders, the police were legally bound to keep him until next morning. 'There were screens at the entrance which showed live images from inside the cells', he remembers, describing the scene as if it belonged to a David Lynch film. 'I imagined myself in one of those cells while the cops prepared to register us.'

Their efforts at locking up Göl and other activists came to nothing, however, when the cops received a call from their superiors instructing them to release the detainees immediately. Feeling greatly relieved, and little aware of what awaited him in the days to come, Göl headed home. In those days, such experiences were truly surprising; in the months to come, they would become ordinary.

Eleven days later Göl learned that the public prosecutor would pursue a civil case against him. He was accused of 'violating the public gatherings law' and noncompliance with the police.

'I am not sure what the legal process would have been like if I was caught during Gezi where people were arrested, and convicted, using the flimsiest of evidence', Göl tells me, describing how his parents calmly took the news about his arrest. 'I called my mother in the first instance and told her I was okay. She said, in a mature voice, that they had the deepest trust in me.'

Göl's parents consider themselves left-wing. They voted against the constitution commissioned by the military dictator Kenan Evren when it was presented to the nation via a referendum on 7 November 1982. They were part of the 8.63 per cent of Turkish citizens who voted against the proposed text. Both chemical engineers, they had met each other in Istanbul while working at the German company Hoechst in the late 1970s.

They sent their only son (they also have a daughter) to the prestigious Robert College, where Göl remembers growing up in a protected environment. There the curriculum's cultural outlook was strongly American: Göl read Faulkner's *As I Lay Dying* and Salinger's *Catcher in the Rye* and had little interest in politics at the time. In 1994, when the Islamist Felicity Party won local elections in Istanbul, this state of affairs changed.

'I remember the atmosphere when they started running Istanbul', Göl tells me. 'There was this fear that the religionists had now taken over the country and that things would be terrible from now on. I remember feeling greatly surprised at the outcome of the elections. People around me said they had not seen anything quite like this before.'

During the 1990s Göl read the dissident comic magazine *LeMan,* which was famous for its lampooning of Turkish police and politicians; carrying a copy while walking on Istiklal Avenue was an act of rebellion.

Göl lived in the upper-middle-class neighbourhood of Gayrettepe with his parents, who started to have fears about their son's increasingly frequent commutes to Taksim. 'During the 1990s Beyoğlu was known as this neighbourhood of pavilions and pimps,' he remembers, 'not a safe place for your son to go regularly.'

Göl decided to study psychology at college and although he never became a practising psychologist (the only exception was during his military service, about which more below), he took advantage of the atmosphere at Bosphorus University, where he befriended a small group of film lovers who came from similar backgrounds and shared his passion for writing about cinema. 'I was not into politics. I was into literature, films and film criticism', he remembers. His new friends shared this mindset; their politicization would take many years to develop.

Before their arrival, Bosphorus University already had a film club and a film magazine named *Görüntü* which was famous for its strongly Marxist take on cinema. The magazine's political reading of films was something Göl and his friends used less in their own writing; they preferred using the tools of film theory alongside a political approach while reading films. Göl remembers how this resulted in their being viewed extremely suspiciously by more senior figures among the university's film circles. 'We felt they considered us bourgeois kids', Göl says. 'Sadly we didn't have much cooperation.'

Göl and his friends were serious about publishing: he joined the film magazine *Altyazı* as an editor two years after it was founded by his Bosphorus friends, during a period when international publications like *Empire* were getting ready to publish Turkish editions and when Turkey's biggest film magazine, *Sinema*, had strong sale figures (both the Turkish edition of *Empire* and *Sinema* have since ceased publication). *Altyazı* was a different venture – independent and addressing a more highbrow, cinephile demographic. It aimed to become a Turkish *Sight & Sound*.

'In its first years *Altyazı* was seen as this magazine that only focused on independent cinema. People considered the magazine harmless. In a sense, there was less reason to be anxious about Turkey in those years.' This changed, however, with the assassination of Turkish Armenian journalist Hrant Dink in 2007. The publisher of the weekly newspaper *Agos*, Dink was assassinated by a young nationalist.

For the first time in its history, *Altyazı* came up with a political message after this event. *Altyazı*'s February 2007 issue featured an image of the slain journalist on its back cover. Thus, the political atmosphere in Turkey had made its way into the protected world of cinema the magazine's publishers had been living in for the previous six years.

'Our biggest struggle was against self-censorship', Göl remembers. Bosphorus University is independent, so the editors never feared external interference, but they did not want to create problems between the magazine and the university administration either. 'We never before published content not directly linked to cinema. But the death of Hrant changed us. We said, "we should go ahead and publish a quote from him". We were anxious about whether the university administration would be irritated by this. On the contrary, they were quite happy with what we did.'

Göl attended Dink's funeral and was somewhat relieved to see that he was not alone. 'Maybe it was an illusion which I re-experienced later at Gezi, this feeling of being part of a multitude', he says. 'In the previous years many of us were armchair leftists, the so-called "children of the 12 September coup" who did not belong to any political organization.' Now they were making their voices heard.

In 2008, after translating books and spending time attending film screenings, Göl started his military service in

Erzincan as part of the Third Army of Turkish Military. 'Half of the population residing at the city centre were soldiers', he says. Göl was a *subay* (officer) and worked as a psychologist; soldiers who had antisocial personality disorders, and those who were inclined to violence, came to him.

This role as army psychologist provided Göl with the opportunity to observe Turkey's youth and their problems – almost all of those who came to him were aged between 18 and 20. 'Some just wanted to avoid physical training exercises. There were self harmers and cutters. My job was to listen and motivate them. I told them things like "everything is going to be alright".'

Göl's position as psychologist was extremely informative. He realized how 'young people lacked the habit of thinking about themselves. They seemed to have never asked themselves the questions "Who am I? What am I? What do I enjoy in life?" It seemed as if nobody had listened to them before in their lives. They were happy just for the fact that I was listening.'

Göl attempted to come up with solutions to their problems but found it to be a most difficult task. 'The stories they told me were often unbearable ... They featured fathers beating their wives, lots of domestic violence. Observing all that was like looking at a large portrait of Turkey. I remember telling myself, "if this is what the youth is like, we are ruined!"'

Upon his discharge from military service, Göl went back to working full time for *Altyazı*, where the editors became more political with every passing day. 'We had this anxiety about where to draw the line between film and politics. We wondered if we could balance the two, and asked ourselves if we wanted to stay as a film magazine. Editors wanted to make political comments but were now wondering whether a film magazine was the proper place for this or whether politics should be done using other channels.'

Göl went to May Day marches in the early 2010s where he walked alongside fellow film journalists and critics. Together they managed to produce alertness and consciousness among readers and followers. He remembers the protest march to save the Emek Theatre as one of the first examples of a social media event that ended up informing people about a real problem in their cities.

'There are two things I clearly remember from early 2013, in the months that led to Gezi', Göl says. 'One is the image of tourists getting tear gassed on Istiklal Avenue during April 2013. The second is a statement made by a leading conservative party figure who said, on 1 April 2013, that their party no longer needed the support of liberal intellectuals who had supported them in the previous years. This new stance against liberals was perhaps not the view of one member but the general view of the party.'

Such developments and realizations shocked many journalists around Göl. When construction machines demolished the Emek Theatre on 20 May 2013, exactly a week before the uprising kicked off, the state of things in Turkey had become much clearer for them. Göl had heard about the news in the offices of *Altyazı*, where he continues to work as an editor. He watched videos of the demolition of the theatre. A week later would come the videos of the burning of tents. Now journalists like Göl felt obliged to step out of the walls of their offices and observe, and experience, the reality that surrounded them on the streets and in Gezi Park.

The image of Göl getting choked by a policeman and his subsequent arrest would create fury among journalists in Turkey. Since 2010, journalists had found themselves in an extraordinary situation. Up until May 2013, what journalists most feared was imprisonment; a 2013 report by the Committee to Protect Journalists pointed out that 'for the second consecutive year, Turkey was the world's leading jailer of journalists, followed closely by Iran and China'. The statistics were nothing less than shocking:

Journalists in Turkish jails declined to 40 from 49 the previous year, as some were freed pending trial. Others benefited from new legislation that allowed defendants in lengthy pre-trial detentions to be released for time served. Additional journalists were freed after CPJ had completed its census on December 1. Still, authorities are holding dozens of Kurdish journalists on terror-related charges and others for allegedly participating in anti-government plots. Broadly worded anti-terror and penal code statutes allow Turkish authorities to conflate the coverage of banned groups with membership, according to CPJ research.

Many of the journalists who found themselves locked up had a shared quality: they were young. Journalists imprisoned in connection with the OdaTV investigation included Barış Pehlivan (born in 1983), Barış Terkoğlu (1980), Coşkun Musluk (1985) and Sait Çakır (1988). They were accused of 'plotting a coup' against the elected government. There was a striking age gap between those young journalists and public prosecutors who went after them and the 'liberal' opinion leaders who supported their imprisonment.

After the momentous summer of 2013, there would be a changed pattern in Turkey's journalism world. Now writers and reporters would begin to fear the prospect of being sacked from their publications, instead of being locked up in Turkish prisons.

A 2015 report published by Harvard Kennedy School's Shorenstein Center on Media, Politics and Public Policy pointed to how Turkey was no longer 'the world's jailer of journalists' at the end of 2014 (the number of imprisoned journalists had fallen to seven, according to CPJ) while the number of sacked journalists has skyrocketed after the Gezi events. According to the report, around a thousand journalists either lost their jobs, were fired or were forced to resign after the uprising. There was something ironic in the shift from the prison cell to the open air. Hundreds of journalists were now 'freed' from their institutions, being advised to change careers.

For senior members of Turkey's press this was by no means unprecedented: they had lost newsroom positions many times in the past. But for the young generation of journalists it was a brutal wake-up call about the state of their country's media scene. This new state of affairs would prove advantageous for some among the young, providing an atmosphere in which they could unleash their potential as journalists. For others it had the more sinister effect of leaving them jobless unless they gave up their political beliefs.

Just consider the case of Berkan Özyer, who found himself in a rather surreal scene on the last day of August 2013. Özyer was in his 1993 model Mazda 323 car, going full speed in the direction of İstinye Park, a shopping mall not far from the offices of the history magazine he had been working for during the past year. Earlier in the day, Özyer, his two colleagues and their editor-in-chief had received some shocking news:

the new issue of their history magazine would not be allowed to go to press. That they were not allowed to publish their new issue came as unpalatable news – but what followed was even more shocking. The publisher was not only cancelling the publication of their new issue; he was closing down the magazine for good.

Censorship is a fact of life for Turkey's journalists, but what Özyer had experienced that day was shocking, even for this formerly half-Sovietic publishing scene.

Before Özyer left the building, his supervisors asked the history magazine crew to hand over their passwords for their Twitter and Facebook accounts immediately. Since the publication was declared dead, it would not be acceptable if it made its voice heard via social media, they had decided.

Alarmed at the prospect of a complete purge of the magazine's content by the administration, Özyer rushed out of the building and headed to the mall where he purchased a hard drive to which the magazine's archive could be digitally transferred, before their team was denied access to it.

Back at the office he copied all the folders containing their page layouts onto the drive; as soon as they saw '100%' on screen, the team breathed a sigh of relief and carefully concealed the drive inside a bag. Weeks later, they would be called to the human resources department where the editorial team was instructed to take a paid rest for a few days and asked about whether they would accept being reallocated to different publications under the same media group – options included a radio station and a website. 'We have shut down the magazine but would not like to see you lose your jobs', they were told. Four of them, including Özyer, rejected the offer.

What had they done wrong? Which factual error had destroyed this history magazine which sold extremely well, having once reached the incredible number of 60,000 monthly sales? (As a former employee of *Newsweek*'s Turkish edition, I remember looking at circulation figures of 5,000 copies for our daily magazine – so 60,000 is pretty huge for a Turkish magazine.)

Özyer had started at the magazine in October 2012, months before the Gezi events. He was happy to work for a magazine whose monthly sales ranged between 35,000 and 40,000 copies. 'It was Turkey's best-selling magazine by a large margin', Özyer tells me in a roadside cafe at Kadıköy, on the Anatolian side of Istanbul, which had been rocked by protests since the Gezi events.

'We didn't get too many ads but the sales figures were more than enough for the magazine to continue with its operations', he remembers. The magazine's formula for success was to offer historical parallels to, and historical readings of, current events. When Prime Minister Recep Tayyip Erdoğan admitted on 23 November 2011 that around 13,000 Kurdish citizens living in the eastern city of Dersim had been massacred by the Turkish military in the 1930s, the magazine devoted a special issue to the massacre, which sold around 35,000 copies. A previous issue, published in 2009, sold 58,000 copies.

Özyer had little idea, in May 2013, that the events at Gezi Park could raise a similar amount of interest among readers. 'I was cynical when the events kicked off', he tells me, lighting a cigarette he has hand-rolled expertly. 'I mocked the protestors, telling myself "oh here they go striking again!"' This cynical attitude would change when a friend of his who went to the park experienced police violence first hand. On 28 May, Özyer saw pictures of a young woman in a red dress getting tear gassed in the face by a riot cop and decided to visit the park.

'Everyone in the magazine headed to the park. We took the most basic spray masks and put those on during the attacks.' Özyer would return to the emptied corridors of their magazine's headquarters after the events, having little idea about the future of the country, or their magazine for that matter. What he knew was that the July issue was due in weeks and that they had to come up with a cover story for it.

The cover story materialized in front of them in the coming days; the answer about what the future issue would be about lay in the present time. Back from the park, Özyer and his editor colleagues made the momentous decision to interpret actuality through history.

'We knew we had to do something about the things that we had been witnessing there. We started planning the July issue on 2 June. It was during this initial meeting that someone came up with the idea of devoting the entire issue to Gezi. We thought about naming it "the extraordinary issue" in a rather tongue-in-cheek way.'

Having decided to devote the entire issue to Gezi and its historical precedents, they realized that even the crossword puzzle could focus on riots and Gezi, if they so wanted. 'Every morning we would work three hours at the office before heading to the park', Özyer remembers. 'It was a bit difficult to do two things at once, but we managed.'

As Özyer and his colleagues prepared for publication, the magazine's editor-in-chief wrote an introductory text in which he was careful neither to endorse the uprising nor support the acts of the police. 'His position was miles away from something like "our heroic people have rebelled against the dictatorship!" The issue's aim was to provide a background to the uprising and look at its precedents in the history of Turkey and the Ottoman Empire, and this is what he said in the editor's note.' Carefully distancing the magazine's stance from both the state and the protestors, the introductory text referred to violence produced by police and protestors in equal measure.

'We asked historians to interpret what was going on in the country', Özyer remembers. 'I was responsible for preparing a timeline of events. We devoted a section to similar movements from other countries. One historian said it was too early to comment; he recommended focusing on the 1950s – it was not the historian's job to comment on events that have occurred after that decade, he said.' They did not follow the historian's advice.

The decision to completely devote the magazine to Gezi would result in huge interest from the public. It resulted, also, in the magazine's closure. 'They saw that the whole magazine was devoted to uprisings around the world; there was no way to censor little elements and edit them out. There was no way to make the issue palatable – thus came the extreme decision to shut down the operation.'

Özyer's mother was born in Bursa and met his father while working for Turkey's state-owned mail and telephone company PTT (the acronym of Post, Telegram and Telephone in Turkish). Both electrical engineers, they served the company for many years as civil servants and led a comfortable life. 'We lived in mass housing buildings that belonged to PTT and paid little rent', Özyer remembers.

Their comfortable existence would change in the 1990s when, under the rule of the centre-right government headed by Turkey's first female prime minister Tansu Çiller and her fellow politician Mesut Yılmaz, a full-scale economic collapse destroyed Turkey's economy, resulting in the devaluation of the Turkish lira, which lost its value massively against the American dollar. This proved problematic for Özyer's family, who had just started paying a mortgage on a new house in American dollars. Like many who earned in lira and owed in dollars, bankruptcy and poverty appeared on the horizon for them. This catastrophe was not only personal but also national: it resulted in the complete destruction of the field of centre-right politics and its conquering by the conservatives.

Özyer's father had a big library filled with books on politics and history. 'I never read novels in my childhood', he confesses. 'I was addicted to books on history and politics.' When he started high school, Özyer befriended pupils who were into politics. 'There were communists, conservatives, nationalists ... and we were excellent friends.' In those years Özyer started visiting the offices of the Turkish Communist Party (TKP) and the Republican People's Party (CHP) – two political parties for which he had sympathy. But after he started college Özyer decided that all parties were the same. There was little sense in spending his time on them.

It was during this time that he attended the first proper political event of his life: the March Against the Invasion of Iraq, organized by Küresel BAK (International Peace Coalition) on 18 March 2006 in numerous cities in Turkey. 'I liked being part of a big crowd', he explains, as young people walk past us in Kadıköy.

Not long afterwards Özyer would realize that the activist's life was not for him. 'Staying at home reading was definitely more enjoyable. Increasingly I came to believe that nothing would change in this country by giving handouts to people and sticking posters on walls.'

At college Özyer studied history and became increasingly suspicious of political activism. 'Things like marching on the streets seemed useless to me. Activists were part of a world isolated from the rest of the country. Whenever we went to a public march we would see the same people. They were chanting the same slogans which reached no one but themselves. They had become their own audience.'

In 2009 Özyer made the unorthodox decision, for a student of history, to become a journalist. He spent his time reading books and gave up his high school habit of hanging out with graffiti artists and painting on the walls of Istanbul. 'My graffiti were hopelessly lame', he admits. 'It was better for me to focus on history.'

Meanwhile Özyer's apolitical stance changed a little when the brother-in-law of one of his close friends got arrested as part of the 'OdaTV investigation', accused by the public prosecutor of being a member of a terrorist organization. 'Journalists who worked for OdaTV were detained for months. And when I looked at the evidence presented against them I was surprised at how absurd it was. The seating chart of a wedding ceremony was presented at court as "the official chart of a terrorist organization". The so-called evidence I had a chance to see was so maddening that I wondered what the rest of the evidence looked like ... In my eyes, the chances of a military coup in Turkey no longer existed and the prospect of a coup was being used as an excuse to lock people up.'

In 2009, with dreams of becoming a journalist and angered by the criminalization of the written word, Özyer started interning for the Turkish edition of *Newsweek* magazine. He quickly became a favourite of his editor; when the IMF chief Dominique Strauss-Kahn visited Istanbul, the job of covering the event fell on Özyer's shoulders.

Strauss-Kahn was scheduled to speak at Bilgi University where Özyer was an undergraduate. As he arrived at the venue, the rector recognized Özyer and wanted to learn whether he would be posing a question to the IMF chief. Özyer saw this as an opportunity and said yes; some minutes later he was placed in one of the conference hall's front seats, so that he could better make his voice heard. After the opening speeches, it was time to ask questions to the IMF chief.

Özyer remembers taking the microphone and starting to formulate a question, in English. 'I was very anxious,' he laughs, 'and so just ran out of English words. I couldn't manage to formulate the question; for a minute and a half, I mumbled some English words in terror, conscious that both my professors in the hall and my editor-in-chief in the *Newsweek* offices were watching me.'

Before Özyer could find a way to finish his question, someone from the back rows threw something at his head. Özyer had little idea what it was that hit him. Reuters' report of the incident, dated 1 October 2009, was titled 'Student throws shoe at IMF chief in Istanbul protest':

A Turkish student threw a shoe at International Monetary Fund Managing Director Dominique Strauss-Kahn on Thursday as he made a speech to students in Istanbul ahead of the IMF's annual meeting.

Security guards dragged the student away after he threw a white sports shoe and rushed towards the stage. The shoe landed at the feet of Strauss-Kahn.

'Get out of the university, thief IMF', he shouted during Strauss-Kahn's speech at Istanbul's Bilgi University. A female student tried to unfurl a protest banner.

Strauss-Kahn shrugged off the incident.

'It is important for us to have an open debate. I was glad to meet students and hear their views. This is what the IMF needs to do, even if not everyone agrees with us, one thing I learned, Turkish students are polite. They waited until the end to complain', he said in a statement.

The incident echoed that of an Iraqi journalist who hurled his shoes, a grave insult in the Muslim world, at then U.S. President George W. Bush last December.

Turkey is hosting the IMF and World Bank annual meetings in Istanbul, which begin on Saturday with meeting of Group of Seven finance ministers.

Up to 30 students started chanting slogans against the IMF and Turkey's AK Party government, such as 'collaborators AKP'. Police detained some of the protesters at Bilgi University.

'He (Strauss-Kahn) is the representative of global capitalism. I tried to raise my views by protesting against him at a time education and health services here have been privatized', student Emre Avci, a member of the Turkish communist party, who was among the protesters, told Reuters.

There is significant opposition among Turkish students to the IMF, which has been involved in protracted talks with Ankara on a major loan agreement.

Security has been stepped up across Turkey's largest city.

Özyer still remembers feeling the shoe of the protestor (who was himself a journalist working for the socialist newspaper *BirGün*) on his head. 'I was glad that it had hit me,' he tells me with a cunning expression on his face, 'otherwise I would not have been able to finish my question.' People still remember

Özyer's desperate attempt to ask a question and getting hit on the head by a white sports shoe. 'They still ask about how it happened when they see me: "Aren't you the guy who was hit in the head, instead of Strauss-Kahn?"' After the incident Özyer was invited to give a number of television interviews. 'I told them I was not the one who had thrown the shoe, I was merely asking a question – why do you want to interview me?'

After his stint at *Newsweek* Özyer started working for the daily *Akşam*, where he was employed on the foreign news desk. 'I was working for this very popular newspaper run by a big conglomerate and soon realized that its foreign desk consisted of two persons: the foreign news chief and myself.' Shortly after Özyer got the job, the foreign news chief retired and the young journalist found himself entirely responsible for the paper's foreign coverage.

During this period Özyer multitasked to the best of his ability: he was editing news stories, translating them, writing analyses, picking photographs, writing subs – pretty much all the things a team of foreign news staffers normally do. After the Turkish government's foreign policy on Syria and Assad changed, Özyer became aware of interference in his coverage from the upper echelons of power. 'Before her retirement, my editor was once sent a set text to be used in our coverage of the crisis in Syria', he says. 'Foreign desks of Turkish papers were strongly influenced by this change in foreign policy.'

Meanwhile Özyer was disappointed about the course of the Ergenekon and Balyoz cases which continued to ruin the careers of numberless journalists and military officers, many of whom said they had no connection with the monstrous events they were accused of orchestrating. 'Those investigations had the potential to cleanse this country's crimes and yet they ended up in a witch hunt', according to Özyer. 'This was profoundly worrying for me.' Although he never feared being locked up himself, the witch hunt atmosphere strongly influenced Özyer's mood. 'I believed that those people, who were so unjustly imprisoned, would be released one day, when the changing of the guard in the Turkish state would already be over.'

After the closing down of the history magazine, Özyer was annoyed to see how all their labour had been for nothing. 'I did not cry', he says. 'The thing is, I was proud of the quality of the content we had produced and was shocked to see it censored this way.'

He need not have worried, since it turned out that censorship didn't really work in their case. Özyer watched numerous people offer the magazine team help in the form of their technical expertise. They would thus be able to publish the content they had transferred to the hard drive on a website. 'One guy said: "Let's do a website!" Another offered to do an app. Finally we agreed to work with this guy who put the entire content of the magazine on the web, using Adobe Flash.'

When Özyer and his sacked friends recently looked at Google Analytics to see how many people have accessed the content of their banned, but not destroyed, history magazine, they were heartened and pleasantly surprised. Hundreds of thousands have reached their 'extraordinary issue', which was proof that the kind of content Turkey's young journalists had been producing in the past years might be, at times, unwanted by media bosses but was not by any means unreachable by those on the lookout for quality content.

Betül Kayahan, an English teacher who had dreams of becoming a feature writer for English newspapers in Turkey, was enjoying a quiet day at her apartment in Istanbul on 11 May 2013 when two car bombs exploded in Reyhanlı, a town on Turkey's border with Syria. Killing 52 people and wounding 140, the attacks were suspected to have been planned by the Syrian intelligence in order to take revenge on Turkey, whose dramatic reconfiguration of its foreign policy, following the Syrian government's brutal repression of its citizens, meant the two neighbouring countries could soon be at war.

Watching horrific images of dead and wounded Reyhanlı residents on TV, Kayahan was deeply unsettled. 'God forbid, something worse will follow this', she said. Her husband, a software engineer from Pakistan, heard her; he was similarly saddened by the news but also seemed irritated by his wife's increasing interest in Turkish politics.

'I had just quit my job as an English instructor and he was not at all happy with that decision', Kayahan tells me in a coffee shop in Gayrettepe, the financial heart of Istanbul, a stone's throw from the headquarters of the English newspaper *Daily Sabah* where Kayahan works as a freelance feature writer.

A week later the couple took a plane far away from Reyhanlı – to Palo Alto, San Francisco, where Kayahan's sister in-law had been living for the last decade. Her sister in-law's husband, the CTO of a software company, welcomed them to Silicon Valley. Kayahan was excited to listen to him talk about their neighbours: executives of leading technology companies, including Facebook, lived around them. They would be spending a month at the heart of technological innovations.

Kayahan is a heavy social media user and so was happy to live close by people whose job it is to create new tools for people like her. They planned to stay in Palo Alto for a month and Kayahan was super excited by the prospect of visiting the campuses of tech companies in Silicon Valley. Shortly after, while trying to take in all these novelties, she received even more exciting news. Her favourite politician, Turkish Prime Minister Recep Tayyip Erdoğan, was in town.

'Turkish PM visits Silicon Valley', ran a headline in *Hurriyet Daily News* on 19 May 2013:

> Erdoğan visited Silicon Valley in San Francisco on May 18 for a tour of leading technology companies.
>
> His first stop was Microsoft, where he was welcomed by CEO Steve Ballmer. Ballmer, who is in charge of the Turkish Education Ministry's Fatih project, briefed the prime minister about the ongoing endeavor. [...]
>
> Later on Erdoğan moved to Apple and Google, where he participated in a test drive of the company's self-driving car along with his daughter Sümeyye Erdoğan and his party's deputy parliamentary group chair, Ayşenur Bahçekapılı.
>
> Google's business development director, Seval Öz, the sister of Mehmet Öz, a well-known Turkish doctor in the United States, briefed Erdoğan on the self-driving car and smart eyeglasses.

'I did not have the slightest idea that Erdoğan was visiting the Valley!' Kayahan tells me. 'My brother-in-law offered to take me to the Google Campus where Erdoğan was scheduled to visit on 18 May.'

In the previous days Kayahan had been surprised at the lack of police cars on Californian streets. On the day of Erdoğan's visit this changed and she saw signs of increased security in the city. Kayahan remembers receiving a text from her mother ('They are now approaching Google') which was another sign that she was on the right track.

Kayahan, her sister-in-law, kids and husband drove to the Google Campus immediately and spent an hour there, taking pictures and walking around different buildings. Kayahan was imagining the moment she would meet Erdoğan. But, even after two hours, the prime minister was nowhere to be seen.

'I had to apologize to my brother-in-law for ruining his day by driving me all the way there', Kayahan remembers. 'It was clear Erdoğan wasn't coming to the campus and so I asked him if he preferred to go back.' Just as she said those words, police cars appeared a few metres away from them. Erdoğan's entourage had arrived and the tall, self-confident politician got out of the car.

'We watched Google's Seval Öz instruct the prime minister about the self-driving Google Car. She then handed him a prototype of Google Glasses. I walked towards him, calling out to him: "Prime Minister! Can I come nearby?" To this he replied: "Oh sure, come nearby." We started chatting, surrounded by cameramen and photographers.'

And what did they talk about? 'Erdoğan asked me about my life in the US, mistaking me for a US-based Turkish woman. I told him we were just visiting. Speaking to Erdoğan I could see how he had an incredible aura. It is as if one could not go near him because of that halo around him.' This was the first time Kayahan had met the politician and memories of this encounter at the Google Campus would stay with her in the following years.

'My respect for him increased greatly after he asked about our life in Turkey. He cared for what we were doing. The following week Erdoğan went back to Turkey and the Gezi uprising began.'

Initially, Kayahan sided with those concerned about the future of Taksim Square. The prospect of a shopping mall constructed in Gezi Park irritated her. 'I believed that the right thing to do was to build back the Ottoman-style military barracks and refashion Taksim Square like the Piazza San Marco in Venice. As for building a shopping mall there, that was something I opposed.' Kayahan thinks the Mayor of Istanbul had mishandled the crisis and had not sufficiently clarified what exactly would be built in the square. 'Things got out of hand because of this ambiguity', she says.

The meaning of the events, however, was very clear for Kayahan, who loves reading history books on the Ottoman Empire. As a prospective journalist, she was quick to draw parallels between the uprising in Gezi and the Young Turks' attempt, in 1908, to usurp the power of Sultan Abdul Hamid II.

'Abdul Hamid II had allowed Young Turks to strip away his power too easily', Kayahan tells me, before taking a sip of her supersized mocha. 'This fact has always made me sad. I read Joan Haslip's *The Sultan: The Life of Abdul Hamid II*, in which the book's British author argues that Abdul Hamid II shouldn't have given up power, adding that had he resisted the pressure of nationalists, and gone to Anatolia in the role of the Caliph, he could have defeated those who wanted to usurp his power.'

For Kayahan, what happened after the uprising in Gezi was not so different from what had happened to Abdul Hamid II; people tried to oust Erdoğan, whose uncompromising stance was what Abdul Hamid II should have shown, so as to keep Ottoman Empire intact.

Although she was angered by the way the Gezi protestors behaved during the uprising, Kayahan admits they have changed her life in a good way, making her dream of becoming a journalist come true. After all, it was during the uprising that she became a more committed user of Twitter. 'People were aware of my anger', she says. 'I was writing very directly and my defence of Erdoğan was very passionate.' When preparations for a conservative-democrat English newspaper supportive of the ruling party began, Kayahan received a call from the editor-in-chief. They agreed on her writing features for the paper on a freelance basis.

'My first essay, published on 1 February, focused on the International Headscarves Day', Kayahan remembers. She then wrote about the love letters of Nelson Mandela. She published essays on Turkey's Ottoman past. After a visit to Andalusia, which left her fascinated by the legacy of Islam, she wrote about how Muslims had translated works by ancient philosophers and spread them to Europe. 'The ideas of Greek philosophers had been introduced to Europe by Muslims but somehow people did not acknowledge that', she tells me. 'Annoyed by Islam's representation in English-language newspapers, I penned my first political article.'

This was not quite what she had in mind when she returned to Turkey from Palo Alto in the summer of 2013, at a time when she had little clarity about her prospects in life. Her desire to correctly represent Islam and its culture in the tumultuous time of the Gezi protests had now turned this young Turkish woman into a journalist.

Kayahan's grandfather was born in Bulgaria and emigrated to the Turkish city of Balıkesir with his family in his adult years. Her mother comes from the Black Sea city of Trabzon. Kayahan was born in Istanbul and still remembers, from her childhood years, the moment her family was forced to make a big decision.

'My father worked in the steel plants industry and had a job offer from Canada', she says. 'We briefly considered moving abroad when I was little. The other option was the city of Ereğli, the home of Turkey's largest steel plant. My father chose not to leave our country.'

Thanks to this choice Kayahan ended up spending her childhood in the beautiful surroundings of a Black Sea city, where she remembers not seeing many conservative families around. 'I remember talking about other families in terms of politics in our household. It was easier to merge with people from different political persuasions in those years.'

Kayahan's grandmother had two brothers. One was a supporter of the entrepreneurially minded Motherland Party (ANAP), one of the ideological ancestors of the AK Party. The other brother was an avid supporter of the Republican People's Party, the statist party which ruled the republic during its initial two decades. Kayahan remembers hearing about and witnessing their discussions at home. 'The leftist brother had instructed my grandmother to vote for the Republican Party in the 1970s but my grandma told me she had secretly voted for the conservatives.'

Under the influence of her grandmother Kayahan developed an interest in the personality of Turgut Özal, the leader of ANAP. She found him a very sympathetic and open-minded figure whose death in 1993 would devastate her.

'I remember playing Lego with a friend in the bedroom when my mother came inside to tell us that Özal has passed away. We did not want to believe her! I felt so terrible and asked myself, "what on earth will happen to this country now?"'

And what did she like about Özal? 'He was a visionary', Kayahan says. 'This chubby man who had lived in the US for many years introduced all kinds of modern stuff to Turkey.' Kayahan's parents were so moved by Özal's death that they left their children at home and went to the deceased president's funeral in Istanbul.

While Turkey's leftists hated him, conservative-minded citizens had adored this US-friendly politician whose struggle to liberalize Turkey's political and economic culture ended up in failure, since his death was followed by the rise of nationalist, statist politics that would be disastrous especially for Turkey's Kurds. But his offering of a mixture of conservative and entrepreneurial values would persevere, and was later adopted by a new wave of conservative politicians.

Kayahan was fascinated by the stories her grandmother told her about how people in the 1940s had to bury their Qur'ans underground so as not to be blacklisted as Islamists under the single-party rule. She told her, too, of her joy at seeing Adnan Menderes and his Democrat Party winning the popular elections in the 1950s. A fan of Erdoğan, Kayahan's grandmother had foretold the politician's rise to power. 'One day she told me, out of the blue, that "Erdoğan will rule Istanbul one day".' When Erdoğan indeed won the mayorship of Turkey's biggest city, Kayahan felt she was in the know. 'What really surprised me in 1990 was the electoral win in the capital Ankara. One day we woke up to the news that both Ankara and Istanbul had been won by people like us.'

After finishing high school Kayahan decided to cover her hair and informed her father about the decision. 'In the 1990s wearing a headscarf was strictly banned in the public sphere. I clearly remember two girls who tried to cover their heads in our school. Every morning our teachers would scold them and this experience had left its mark on me. I told my father about this, saying I wanted to study elsewhere. He offered to send me to a boarding school where I could freely cover my hair.'

Wearing the headscarf and going to a boarding school would change pretty much everything in Kayahan's life. First, she had to part from her parents; from now on she would study at a private boarding school where she would be surrounded by a group of girls who would become her best friends.

'There were four of us and we were really perfect friends. We spent our time interviewing each other. We acted like journalists ... One of us would play the role of the secularist republican, while others personified liberal and conservative figures.' Kayahan loved this 'theatre of opinions' and remembers me how their 'plays' would almost always be about current events.

The girls' interest in media and public debate was reflected in their enthusiasm for the radio shows of Beyazıt Öztürk, a popular left-wing radio host whose programmes were aimed at sleepless Turks on the lookout for some intelligent talk after hours.

'He used to play left-wing songs from political bands and talk about current events. We started sending faxes to him', Kayahan remembers with a smile on her face. 'We wanted him to hear our thoughts.' Öztürk's radio show would run from 10 p.m. to 1 a.m. 'The faxes we sent to him were signed GRUP ZÖ. We wrote our messages in the daytime and sent them before midnight', Kayahan says, as if describing the rituals of a secret society.

Those years turned out to be formative for her group of friends. Kayahan realized how much she enjoyed socializing with others and how self-confident she had become since she was allowed to live with her friends, away from the restrictions of the state. 'I really liked meeting new people; I could talk to them for hours on end', she says.

In those years Kayahan and her friends had big dreams. 'We wanted to go to America and live there for a while', she says. Then came the military coup of 28 February 1997; suddenly, conservative girls like Kayahan and members of her entourage were demonized in the public sphere. From now on they would not be allowed to pursue academic degrees unless they dressed exactly the way the state wanted them to.

Kayahan had wanted to be a journalist from an early age but was told that it was not a career worth pursuing. The doors of the media were closed to conservative people, she learned from her uncle-in-law, a journalist who warned her about the problems female journalists had in the media. Convinced that journalism was not her cup of tea, Kayahan decided to pursue a career in teaching English.

But where would she study? She heard from friends that Gazi University in Ankara allowed girls to wear headscarves, thanks to the institution's conservative-nationalist ideology. 'People said I wouldn't face any problems there.' Kayahan's best friend, meanwhile, enrolled at Istanbul University. There she was forced to enter the 'Persuasion Rooms', created by the ultra-secular administration with the aim to persuade veiled students. Students like Kayahan were required to enter specially designed rooms where their professors instructed them about the importance of changing their lifestyles and replacing their garments so as to be allowed to continue living in the country. If the student accepted their diagnosis and indeed changed her garments (i.e. removed her veil) she would be allowed to enter a door leading to the university corridors. If she refused, her academic life would come to an end and she would be asked to exit from another door that led to the street.

After the traumatic experience of being forced into a Persuasion Room, Kayahan's best friend, along with many others like her, fled the country and enrolled at a university in the US. The big trauma of the Persuasion Room and the subsequent loss of her right to an education would be followed by a new life in the US. This was, in a weird way, the fulfilment of their high school dreams of living in the US, although not in the manner they had imagined.

At Gazi University in Ankara, Kayahan had to deal with a subtler version of discrimination. 'We did not have much problem with male professors,' she remembers, 'but leftist-Kemalist female professors really picked on us. It was strange to see women professors behaving this way. I remember one summer day, when I was wearing a headscarf, how one of them came near me in class and started looking at my body. I was wearing sandals. She said: "oh, dear, don't you feel *cold* in those sandals?" And I was like, "no, why should I be *cold* when the weather is this hot?" Of course, what she meant was that I was wearing a headscarf and sandals together, which, for her, was contradictory.'

Although her grades were among the highest in class, Kayahan could see how she was treated differently, just because she wore the veil. 'Once I got 98 out of 100 in an exam. I had prepared for it with a friend who got 92. Our professor congratulated her for the extremely high grade. When she saw my paper, she lifted her head, and seeing that I wore a headscarf, just handed me the paper and moved on to the next student. This was a subtle version of discrimination.'

Less subtle versions of the same discrimination would arrive soon – the next year in fact, when Kayahan was told that she would not be able to enter the university premises with her headscarf any longer. Kayahan found a solution to this in the form of wearing hoodies which allowed her to cover her hair and enter the school premises. Suddenly, school corridors were filled with hoodie-wearing young girls, who would remember what had been imposed on them for many years to come.

'I would remove my headscarf in a lavatory, just outside the entrance. I would then wear my hoodie and enter the building.' Kayahan had not wanted to cause problems for anybody: 'I just tried merging into the new environment', she says. This would include taking off her veil towards the end of her education. 'Once a professor saw me putting on the veil after the end of the class. She looked at me and said: "oh dear, I never knew you were like this!" She looked as if she was deceived.'

One of her closest friends at college was the daughter of a military commander. During the first year, they used to sit in the front row during class. After the introduction of the headscarf ban, Kayahan felt uncomfortable in her new outlook and would take refuge in the back seats. 'This is an unacceptable situation, we should let Betül wear whatever she likes', her friend protested in class. But the restrictions were strict and impossible to ignore.

Stories about what had happened to girls who insisted on wearing the veil continued to irritate, and shock, Kayahan. A veiled student had entered class one day, only to be rebuked by her professor for not following university rules. 'But this is my constitutional right, sir, I have the right to an education!' the girl protested. 'That may be correct, but you should remember that we have the right not to be with you in the same classroom', the professor replied. Taking all the other students with her on the way to another classroom, she left the veiled student there.

Kayahan was scared to fly back to Istanbul after watching images of the uprising on TV. 'While watching CNN's coverage of the uprising, I hoped that the prime minister would not compromise. It was not about Erdoğan, after all, it was about creating chaos and turning Turkey into a country like Syria.'

While in San Francisco, she had been talking with her mother, asking her whether she should stay in the US. 'I believed something similar to the 28 February coup was taking place in Turkey. I knew that people like me would be the first to go, if the coup was successful.' Since she had defended the state in her tweets during that tumultuous summer, Kayahan was scared she might have been placed on the list of 'first to be arrested'. 'I thought I would get arrested once we returned to Turkey. It was like entering a tunnel where you experience things more intensely.'

Passionate about her defence of the government, Kayahan took to Twitter. 'I was shocked to see the extent of disinformation spread by protestors', she says. 'There were fake, Photoshopped images of burnt youths, bullets purportedly used by cops ... I took a stance against this disinformation campaign. If you don't do that, even the most rational people start believing in those lies.'

After returning to Istanbul, Kayahan saw that there was little to worry about: the conservatives continued to remain in power. She was heartened by the uncompromising stance of Erdoğan. 'He didn't allow chaos to reign in this country.'

Nevertheless Kayahan accepts that the government should do more to make secularists feel at ease in their country. 'There are those who intensely hate Erdoğan. But then there are those who are genuine in their fears about the future of our country. They can even vote conservative in the future. Those people should be reassured about their safety.' She says she had been expecting this kind of conflict: 'Since graduating from college I was surprised that people had not done this kind of thing before. I was like, "how do they manage to repress their anger?" I have seen so much anger in people around me and I was curious about how they had suppressed it in the past.'

Kayahan watched the ousting of Mohammed Morsi in the first days of July 2013. Seeing images of Egypt's first elected prime minister behind bars only strengthened her belief that what Turkey had almost experienced was similar. 'The danger we had lived through here was caused by police violence', she says. 'Just think: why should Erdoğan have given the order to burn the tents of those protestors at the park? He did the complete opposite, and invited protestors to tell him what they wanted to say. But then what did some of those people say to him? They said they didn't want the new airport or the new bridge ... My husband, who is no big fan of the government, was shocked to hear those demands and asked me why on earth had those protestors not wanted to live in a more advanced and civilized city.'

Kayahan had attracted the fury of numerous Twitter users because of her passionate defence of the government through social media. 'I was lynched numerous times on Twitter', she says. 'I received death threats. People said they would hang me in Taksim Square. There were rape threats, too.' She had no other option but to freeze her account for a few months.

Since the incident, Kayahan says she has become accustomed to empathizing with people who have been lynched on social media because of their opinions, however inflammatory they may be. When Turkish singer Leman Sam, famous for her distaste for conservatives, compared the Islamic sacrifice of lambs during religious festivities to atrocities committed by the so-called Islamic State, Kayahan knew what Twitter had in store for the singer.

'If I had not been lynched myself, I would perhaps mention her in an angry tweet', she says as lunch break approaches, with dozens of office workers rushing into our coffee shop to buy sandwiches, snacks and salads. 'Having lived through all the horrors of lynching, I felt an urge to protect her', Kayahan says. 'I wanted to tell people, "please don't call her names, don't swear at her parents, don't threaten her with violence and abuse".' The new climate of anger in Turkey has transformed this pious young journalist into the defender of unbelievers who, only 15 years ago, attempted to deny people like her their right to education.

One fine day in March 2014, Turkish journalist Sibel Oral was working in her office when her editor-in-chief approached her table with an irritated expression on his face. She was surprised to see him walking frantically around her desk, drawing circles and not saying a word, although clearly preparing to. 'Are you busy?' he asked finally. 'No', came the reply. 'Want to chat in my office a bit?' 'Sure', Oral said. She got up and left her desk with little idea that this would be her final hour on the newspaper. She was about to be sacked.

Inside the office, Oral's editor asked his young colleague

to take a seat. He walked towards his desk, where printouts of screen-captures of tweets Oral had been sending over the previous weeks waited inside a dossier. He started showing them to her; in the most recent tweet, Oral had referenced 'Çektir Git', a rock song by the band Mavi Sakal (Blue Beard) which made a name for itself during the 1990s with its rebellious lyrics and uplifting rock tunes. In Turkish, the title of 'Çektir Git' is a variation of the expression 'fuck off' ('*siktir git*'). In her tweet Oral had used the expression while addressing the Turkish prime minister, whom she referred to by his initials.

'Did you write this tweet?' Oral heard her editor ask about the potentially libellous message. 'Yes', Oral replied, feeling unsettled by the experience. She was sitting on a chair, not knowing what would happen next.

'What have you done?' he continued, his head between his hands. 'When I hired you, I warned you that this is a conservative newspaper.'

'But these tweets contain my personal views', Oral said. 'This is my Twitter feed where I can express whatever I like.'

'Express what you want but the administration does not want to work with you any longer', she was told.

'What on earth does that mean?' Oral asked. 'Is that it? Am I sacked?'

She was.

'I was in deep shock', Oral tells me in a trembling voice. I can see she is close to tears even while recounting the scene. We are in the offices of the Platform for Independent Journalism, known here as P24, founded in 2014 to 'support and promote editorial independence in the Turkish press at a time when the journalistic profession is under fierce commercial and political pressure'. Oral is sitting behind the desk of Hasan Cemal, the veteran journalist and founding president of P24 who, in his youth, had defended an army-backed coup against the elected government.

In the past, Oral had worked with some of the other founding members of the platform (including journalists Yasemin Çongar and Andrew Finkel) while she was the culture editor of the liberal newspaper *Taraf* from 2009 to 2012.

'I asked the editor whether it was not absurd that I was getting sacked over a tweet', Oral remembers. 'In my time at *Taraf*, I was allowed to tweet against that newspaper's editorial line and nothing would happen to me after voicing my opinions.'

Upon leaving her editor's office Oral returned to her desk and put on her headphones. She played a song by the Turkish band Büyük Ev Ablukada ('The Big House under Siege') whose song 'Çıldırmayacağım' ('I Will Not Go Crazy') she had made a habit of listening to in stressful times. Soon afterwards, she started packing her belongings and left the building, never to return.

By evening that day, Oral's friends in the media who had been notified of her sacking started publishing articles about her ordeal. In the following days she would give numerous interviews and pen her own account of what had happened. She was featured in a documentary about the sacking of Turkey's leading journalists; Reporters Without Borders got into touch, as did a reporter from a French radio station; she was interviewed by an Italian women's magazine. In all these interactions Oral was frequently asked the question: 'Why were you sacked?'

Not long after, she began to feel irritated by the question before getting a bit tired of all the interview requests. 'It is a good thing that people care about you,' she says, 'but I was also curious about why they were queuing up to create this hero out of me. I was aware that this role, which they appointed to me, would last only a few days. Then I would need to address a more pressing question which concerned my life – about how I would be able to pay next month's rent.'

Oral's mother had lived in Germany before coming to Turkey at the age of 20. There she had met Oral's father, from whom she separated after three years of marriage, before returning to Germany. In Istanbul Oral stayed with her father who owned a record shop in the city's Çağlayan neighbourhood.

'It was a very tiny shop, with enough space only for two people', Oral tells me. 'He was selling audio cassettes. Then he shifted his focus to CDs. Later he expanded the store and turned it into a boutique, selling women's and men's clothes. It was the era before shopping malls – a good time to make money from selling clothes in a small shop.'

At the time Çağlayan neighbourhood was attracting immigrants from the eastern cities. Its population started to include Turks, Kurds and Arabs; it was quickly becoming a cosmopolitan place. Oral remembers her father playing songs by Led Zeppelin and Pink Floyd from his little shop, while she watched the faces of passing pedestrians, trying to guess their feelings about 1970s rock.

Oral shared her father's taste in music. 'He was a Zeppelin kind of guy. My mother was more into Rod Stewart. She was more nationalist, perhaps because of her experience of living in Germany as a Turkish woman. My father, meanwhile, is more of a leftist-republican.'

Oral's father dropped out of high school because of his distaste for authority. A big reader of literature, he was so irritated by school discipline that he decided to get on the nerves of his professors. At the age of 15 he started growing a beard and refused to have his hair cut. He was eventually forced to leave school. 'Because of this he left home and went to Istanbul's Sultanahmet neighbourhood where he lived in tents with hippies', Oral says.

Despite his rebellious attitude, her father, showed little interest in politics. Oral describes him as a Kemalist: 'The only newspaper he allowed to enter our apartment was *Cumhuriyet,* the leading representative of that ideology', she says. 'He is a member of the Atatürkist Thought Association. Our big trauma was the assassination of *Cumhuriyet* columnist and investigative journalist Uğur Mumcu in 1993. My father attended the funeral and brought a framed picture of Mumcu back home. It is still there, I believe.' Like many prospective young journalists, Oral was traumatized by Mumcu's killing by a car bomb, drawing a subconscious parallel between investigative journalism and the assassination of those who practise it.

Oral spent her childhood living with her father who had by then cut his hair and had more children from his second marriage. As he learned to fit more into Turkish society, his daughter would feel alienated from it.

'I used to spend all my time indoors, at home', she says. Alarmed, her father enrolled Oral at a school where she could better socialize with other pupils. But once the academic season began, she realized this school would have an unsettling effect on her life. It was 1993, the year of the Sivas massacre, where 35 writer friends of Aziz Nesin were burned to death when their hotel was torched by an Islamist mob. 'At school we had this religion professor called Mikhail. One day in class, he started commenting on the Sivas massacre and fantasized about "the atheist writer Nesin being torn to pieces". His preferred tool for this operation was a nail clipper. I was shocked to hear that such things could be said at school, but remained silent. A few weeks later, he started talking politics again. He lectured us about the importance of wearing burqas. This time I lost control and got up from my seat. "These may be your ideas and you may want to express them in class but we are not required to listen to them", I said.' His response to Oral's protest was simple: he kicked the young girl out of class but chose not to report her to the administration. In the following days, Oral expressed her protest of her treatment in that class by refusing to recite verses from the Qur'an. Then strange things began happening to her.

One day, Oral's father received a phone call. The voice on the other end of the line started reading verses from the Qur'an without telling him why he was doing such a thing. A few days later, Oral found a little paper note in the pocket of her coat in school. It was a letter asking her to mind her manners and treat the religion professor properly so as not 'to end up like that journalist Mumcu'.

Showing the note to her father that evening, Oral was surprised to hear his theory about how all the things that had been happening to her in the past month were somehow connected: her protest at class, the phone calls, the handwritten note – there surely was a thread that connected all these. 'You should keep your ideas to yourself', he instructed Oral, adding: 'You don't have to be outspoken all the time.' 'But this is how you have raised me', Oral objected. 'Just take it easy for a while', came the answer.

Three weeks after their talk, Oral was walking in the European neighbourhood of Balmumcu to meet a friend with whom she had planned to study for the maths exam scheduled to take place that afternoon. As she neared her friend's house someone suddenly grabbed her from behind. A hand was placed on her mouth; something sharp cut her flesh. It was a rainy day and she remembered one of the attackers, who had a beard, losing his balance and falling down. She escaped from them and took refuge in her friend's house where, covered in blood, she telephoned her father.

They rushed to the police station, filed a complaint, went to a hospital to get a medical report and visited the school administration the next day to tell them about how the events had progressed and how they could have all been related to the religion professor. Meanwhile her father telephoned the offices of *Cumhuriyet*, where the editors invited the young girl to come to the newspaper to talk about her ordeal.

'I was 16 and I wanted to be a journalist and there I was, at the heart of a story that *Cumhuriyet* wanted to cover', Oral remembers. When she went to their offices, Oral talked openly about her desire to become a journalist. 'So here is your chance, Sibel, why don't you write your first piece for us?' she was told. Her father objected, saying it would only bring more trouble. She decided to write her story under a pseudonym.

As soon as the piece was published, Oral started receiving invitations to talk shows. Meanwhile her professor was investigated by the school administration. But the stress of her ordeal cost her an academic year, since she failed many of her classes.

The same pattern re-emerged at high school where Oral was annoyed by a literature professor who 'constantly talked about Mehmed the Conqueror', the Ottoman sultan best known for conquering Istanbul. Oral says he had plans to build a *masjid*, the Islamic prayer room, inside the school premises; in the eyes of her younger, angrier self, the way he presented himself at school was unacceptable and needed interference from outside.

Oral remembers having rushed out of his class twice in anger. She told other pupils to join her protest. One day she took her political activities one step further by way of bringing to class a sound recorder. The plan was to secretly tape the professor's speech. This she did before mailing the tapes to the ministry of education. In full protest mode Oral also took on the job of spraying slogans on school walls. She remembers one of the slogans she wrote, one that was a favourite among Kemalists at the time: 'Turkey will never turn into Iran!' – implying that people would not allow a regime change in the country, from a secular state to one ruled by shari'a.

These activities would prove costly: Oral was suspended from school. 'Thanks to my suspension I ended up hating school and my professors', Oral says. The same year her closest friend in high school committed suicide, which only deepened her distress. 'I was 17, and devastated', she tells me. 'I didn't see the point of continuing with my education.'

After her graduation Oral worked in numerous jobs from bartending to selling tickets for a private theatre. In the noughties she started her journalistic career. Interestingly, it was the editor who would sack her many years later who gave her her first job and educated her about being a proper newspaper reporter.

In 2009 Oral started working as a culture reporter for a small liberal newspaper called *Taraf*, which in the following years would turn into arguably the most controversial, and influential, newspaper in Turkey.

Founded in 2008 by novelist Ahmet Altan and seasoned journalist Yasemin Çongar, *Taraf* was famous for its anti-militarist stance and support for the investigations of military personnel, politicians and, later, journalists suspected of having planned a coup against the elected government. Strongly disliked by nationalists and socialists for its ultra-liberal stance and continuous scrutiny of Kemalism, the newspaper's revelations during the so-called Balyoz (Sledgehammer) and Ergenekon investigations earned it numberless enemies in the country.

Most damagingly, the newspaper was an ardent supporter of the infamous OdaTV case which resulted in the locking up of dozens of journalists, turning Turkey into the biggest jailer of journalists in the world. The day after the arrests of journalists *Taraf* ran a headline that read: 'They were not imprisoned because of journalism', associating journalistic activities with terrorism.

Oral was very critical of *Taraf*'s stance in those investigations. At the same time, she admired its courageous reporting of human rights abuses by state officials. Working there proved to be a transformative experience: growing up in a republican family who considered *Cumhuriyet* as the only acceptable newspaper, it came as a shock for her father to hear that she worked for *Taraf*, whose scrutiny of the very foundations of the republic earned it a reputation as an anti-republican paper.

'The chief of the General Staff was an important figure in our household', Oral remembers. 'I was now working for a paper that made fun of him, telling him his place when the general opposed the policies of the prime minister.'

During her time at *Taraf* Oral was responsible for editing two pages of culture and arts every day of the week. No other paper devoted that much space to cultural coverage. 'In the eyes of our editors, coverage of culture was more important than the coverage of politics', Oral says. 'I was subsequently offered to edit the paper's book supplement, which proved to be a fascinating experience. During the three and a half years I spent there I learned an awful lot – not only about journalism but also about life.'

Although she worked as the paper's culture editor and was responsible for preparing its monthly book supplement, Oral had a very modest income. In order to make ends meet, she freelanced for other publications. There were days when she didn't have money in her bank account; after editing the first issue of *Taraf*'s book supplement she went home in the wee hours of the day and, turning on the heater, realized that her gas had been cut off since she didn't have enough money in her account to pay the bill. 'I remember crying that evening. I was mad for being poor but I was also ecstatic to have produced a magazine that people were very curious to read.'

Oral's happy days at *Taraf* would come to a sudden end on 14 December 2013 when her editor Çongar asked the staff to meet in one of the newspaper's conference rooms. There she talked at length about the problems editors were facing in their relationship to the newspaper administration. Ahmet Altan had already left his post, and took refuge in his home, where he was writing his new novel (titled *Endgame*, it was published by Canongate Books in Britain in 2015).

'We are both leaving the paper and we wanted to let you know', Çongar told the *Taraf* staff. 'You are absolutely free to continue working here but for us, the *Taraf* adventure is over.' When she finished her speech, Çongar (who had left behind her life in Washington to come to Istanbul and start *Taraf*) was in tears.

Oral and a few colleagues close to the novelist went out to meet Ahmet Altan at a cafe where they discussed future prospects for the team. Altan told them that the administration had asked them to tone down their political critiques in the paper. At the office an hour later, Oral had already made up her mind: she would resign from *Taraf*. She left all her belongings in the office and walked out of the building with just a handbag. She has not returned to that building again.

'Once I stepped onto the pavement I felt very good', she says.

By early 2014, Oral was jobless, after her resignation and sacking. She had more than enough time to realize how angry she was about the goings-on in Turkey. Oral was particularly sensitive about the Roboski airstrike incident of 2011, where Turkish F16 jets killed 34 smugglers, mistaking them for PKK terrorists. 'I could see how mainstream media was covering up what had happened there', Oral says. 'I was outraged equally by what the Turkish military had done there and how Turkish media was doing its best to cover it up.'

Two months after her sacking from *Akşam* Oral finally felt ready to do something new. 'The past few weeks had been miserable. Eventually I decided that another kind of journalism was possible and that I would be the one practising it.' And how would she afford to produce this new kind of journalism about the Roboski incident, as a freelancer? 'I needed money and time. I told Yasemin about my project. She advised me to apply for a journalistic grant.' Oral wrote a proposal, which was accepted, and planned to divide her book into three parts: what had happened in Roboski, what people who had lived through the bombing told her, and how Turkish media reported the incident.

Oral feared, before leaving Istanbul, that on her return people would not believe her and accuse her of 'agitation' because of the book. That was, after all, what her mother had told her while questioning her about the project. 'She asked me not to go to Roboski', Oral remembers. 'She said they would manipulate me. "They will exaggerate their experiences and you will believe and write all of them", she said. I felt so angry at those words. I mean, "exaggerate", come on! I asked her what she meant by "exaggerate": "How can you *exaggerate* your experiences when decomposed parts of your son's body are found under a rock on a hill? How can you *exaggerate* when your husband's body has melted into that of a mule, by the power of the bomb?" She accused me of looking at things from an emotional and one-sided perspective. "Why don't you take into account what soldiers have lived through there?" she asked.' Finally, she threatened to disown Oral if she went to Roboski and wrote the book.

Oral did not care. On 1 August 2014, she found herself in the south-eastern city of Cizre, located on Turkey's border with Syria and populated by Turks, Kurds and Assyrians. There she was welcomed by journalist colleagues who showed her around the city that still bore witness to the civil war of the 1990s between the Turkish state and Kurdish militants. Apartment facades were covered with bullet holes, people were poor, the military presence continued to create tension between authorities and armed youth groups. Before travelling from Cizre to Roboski, Oral covered her hair with a veil and made sure to appear 'traditional'. 'It was the hottest days of the year, in August, and I wore long trousers and long-sleeved shirts. I hid my tattoos and hair so as to better reach them.'

For nine days Oral lived in an alternative world, one that was very different from the newspaper offices where she had spent her life in Istanbul. 'I started questioning my life, and asked myself why I was living so isolated from the rest of the country.' She witnessed daily blackouts, saw the difficulty of accessing clean water, and was irritated, like locals, by the constant necessity to provide one's identity card on the streets. Her intention was to interview relatives of the Roboski incidents alone, without any intermediaries: she took notes, lived in their houses, but was unable to write anything. 'I was utterly depressed. I couldn't concentrate on anything.' Her interviewees told Oral chilling stories. One lady described burying the legs of her son three days after the funeral. With the legs separated from her son's body by the force of F16 bombs, she had to bury them in a separate grave.

'How can you ask questions to people who had lived such things?' Oral asks me rhetorically.

Oral returned to Istanbul and spent the following six months writing and rewriting her book. She did her best to narrate using an unsentimental voice and approach the issue objectively. Maybe this was the effect of her mother's warnings made before her journey to Roboski.

While writing the book, Oral's mother had not once phoned her. The day after the publication of *Toprağın Öptüğü Çocuklar* ('Children Kissed by Earth') Oral visited her in her apartment.

It was a calm and eventless meeting. Mother and daughter spent the day silently, not talking about their past disagreements, watching television. As she started preparing to leave the house, Oral realized that her mother had fallen asleep. She looked at her face and watched her for a moment. She took her book out of her bag, signed it and placed it on the table by the bed. She closed the door and left the house.

'This was my "thank you" to her. I realized that I had written my book for people like her.'

A few days later, her nationalist mother posted a photograph of the signed fly-page of Oral's Roboski book on her Facebook wall. She wanted all her friends and relatives to see that she was proud of her daughter.

In Turkey there is much anger waiting to be represented in the mainstream media. But who decides which type of anger is fit to print is anybody's guess. Once upon a time, in the 1990s, printing pictures of headscarved girls fighting for their right to education was an extremely dangerous act. I learned about this thanks to a dramatic event in my university years. The private college I attended was allowing headscarved girls to enter the university premises, and there were numerous prospective journalists at the college campus whose headscarves later got them into serious trouble.

In 2002 the Turkish newspaper *Hürriyet,* a staunch opponent of women's right to wear headscarves in public spaces, published on its front page a photograph from a lecture room in my university that showed headscarved girls in the audience. Only a few days later, the school banned the girls from entering the school premises. Most of our friends were forced to drop out of college and go to live abroad; for those who stayed, we made audio recordings of lectures and they would wear wigs during the exams.

Nowadays, it is the image of angry protestors that typically gets publishers and broadcasters into trouble. Kurdish journalists continue to be killed in war-torn cities in Turkey's south-east. In Istanbul and Ankara, the government has been taking over numerous media groups. In October 2015, a broadcaster affiliated to Islamist cleric Fetullah Gülen's 'Hizmet' movement was seized on air; the editors of the station locked themselves inside the broadcast room where they reported on what they termed 'the siege' of their building as it was surrounded by cops who wanted to enforce a court order to confiscate the company. Hours later, cops made their way into the control room and viewers could watch the event as an officer pushed away the editors and turned off the camera.

For young journalists, there is much to report on and analyse in New Turkey. More than reporting the news, newspapers and broadcasters have become the news here, as they had been throughout the past century. From Hasan Fehmi in the 1900s to Uğur Mumcu in the 1990s to Hrant Dink in the 2000s, almost every decade has had its journalistic martyr. For today's youth, journalism remains a dangerous occupation and people are searching for ways to do their jobs without facing persecution.

Three months after our interview, Sibel Oral was busy editing the next issue of K24, a new cultural magazine that focuses on culture and takes the *New York Review of Books* as its model.

Berke Göl was equally busy, putting the final editorial touches to the October 2015 issue of *Altyazı* magazine while continuing to tweet about the political issue that has been infuriating him the most lately: the rekindled armed conflict between Kurdish militants and the Turkish state, which resulted in violent confrontations between two sides in Cizre, a city where support for an armed uprising is high.

Over e-mail Berkan Özyer told me about his new work environment: he is now an editor at a magazine focusing on climate change, ecology and green technologies. 'It is a small magazine populated by good people. Therefore it pays very little and I am on the lookout for small freelance jobs that I can do in my spare time.' Özyer concluded his e-mail by telling me about his decision to change careers and move on to academia. 'I gave up my journalistic hopes', he wrote.

When I last spoke to her, Betül Kayahan was over the moon about Jeremy Corbyn's win in the UK Labour Party leadership election. Delighted with Corbyn's support for Palestine and his history with political organizations like Hamas, Kayahan's only fear was that the new Labour leader could be ousted by the British army. In late September 2015, the *Sunday Times* newspaper reported on senior British military officers' horror at Corbyn's election and their threat of a possible coup in case Corbyn became prime minister of Britain. 'Brits have openly supported Sisi's coup in Egypt in 2013,' Kayahan tweeted recently, 'and I wouldn't be surprised if they managed to make a coup in Britain too.' She seemed worried about the international press treating Corbyn the same way they treated Mohammed Morsi in Egypt and Recep Tayyip Erdoğan in Turkey.

# CHAPTER FOUR

# Rise of Turkey's Angry Young Entrepreneurs

The Turkish state and industrialists are twins born in the same instant, during the foundation of the secular republic in the 1920s. They grew up, prospered and transformed the country together, rarely leaving each other's company. The Turkish state was founded on corporatist principles: the industrialist and the statesman worked hand in hand, belonging to the same elite circles and forging the country in their image. During two decades of single-party rule, between 1922 and 1945, membership of the state apparatus meant unchecked power, limitless influence and future prospects for the businessman. An industrialist couldn't afford to fall out with the state, otherwise he would lose everything. The Turkish state discouraged free enterprise and competition, instead rewarding those most loyal to its machinations.

The most successful industrialist of the Turkish republic, Vehbi Koç, was 16 when he started working at a grocery store in Ankara. He was 27 when he became the Turkish representative of Standard Oil and Ford Motor Company. As the republic moved the capital from Istanbul to Ankara, Koç continued to prosper and took advantage of the rapidly growing construction and building industries. As the republic built new roads, houses and institutions with its firm grip on political power, it became an increasingly profitable occupation to move forward with it. And this is exactly what Koç's generation of entrepreneurs did.

In the 1940s, with the introduction of Varlık Vergisi (Wealth Tax), Turkey's non-Muslim citizens (Armenians, Levantines, Greeks and Jews) were ordered to pay inordinately higher rates of tax. While Muslims were paying around 5 per cent tax, Jewish citizens were asked to pay an incredible 179 per cent tax; Christian Armenians, meanwhile, had to pay a staggering 232 per cent.

Until its abolition in 1944, the law meant financial ruin for Turkey's minorities, many of whom committed suicide or were forced to flee the country. Those who could pay the required taxes, in 15 days in cash, were forced to sell their properties for very low prices at public auctions. As for those who were not able to come up with the required tax in cash, they were sent to Kop Pass and Aşkale labour camps. There, members of the minority groups, most of whom were elderly, were forced to work all day, accompanied by Turkish soldiers who were ordered to control them. This was an era when numerous members of Turkey's ruling party, the People's Republican Party (CHP) and those in the upper echelons of the General Staff were more openly supporting the policies of the Third Reich and asking Turkey to take the side of Adolf Hitler's party in the war.

Varlık Vergisi cost the lives of 21 people who died in the labour camps. As they, and countless others, vanished into distant Anatolian labour camps, the companies and properties of those wealthy citizens were confiscated by the state. Now Turkey's young Muslim entrepreneurs were offered an excellent opportunity to make a quick buck. Vehbi Koç took advantage of the situation, purchasing those buildings in public auctions; he grew his company massively in the 1940s, signing agreements with General Electric, importing cars from the Fiat company and signing an agreement with Ford

Motor Company. When Koç retired in 1984, his company had already turned into one of Turkey's leading global companies: it employed 80,000 people and had around $40 billion turnover.

Young industrialists of the past century, like Koç, were expert importers of foreign technologies. As the state's handmaidens, their role consisted of assembling parts of foreign-produced materials, be they cars or refrigerators. Attila İlhan, one of Turkey's most important poets and intellectuals from the past century, christened them the *comprador bourgeoisie.* Members of this indigenous middle-class movement had connections to multinational corporations and foreign investors and relied heavily on the state apparatus; İlhan accused them and Turkey's establishment of destroying the national economy and making Turkey dependent on foreign capital.

Today's young entrepreneurs seem to agree with İlhan's analysis. Many of them belong to a new entrepreneurial class called 'Anatolian tigers' whose rise to prominence began in the 1980s, in cities including Gaziantep, Kayseri, Bursa and Kahramanmaraş.

As young protestors in Istanbul started occupying parks and marching in squares, some business people joined them and took to the streets. This was strange, given the Occupy-like nature of the protests – it's not every day you see young business people marching with activists who want to do away with capitalism. Meanwhile, many conservative entrepreneurs sided with the government, interpreting the events as part of a foreign-controlled coup. Once again, Turkey's young people were divided in politics but united in their passion.

※

Almost all of the people I talked to for this book have courage, youth and a gift for articulating their ideas. What most of them don't have is money. They have some money but not large amounts of it. My interviewees so far have been either unemployed graduate students or wage earners or entry level politicians. All of them were unmarried when I talked to them. So the money they earn is to support themselves only. The risks they took while participating in Turkey's political sphere (be it in the anti- or the pro-government camp) concerned only themselves.

Things are slightly different when one has courage, youth, a gift for articulation *and* millions to lose. A Turkish journalist can become a 'freedom hero' when she loses her job and lecture about the experience for the rest of her life; oppression can turn a dissident artist into a profitable investment for the gallery that represents him abroad; but a business person blackballed in the eyes of the government of the country in which she operates runs the risk of no longer being able to function as a business person. This was the reasoning behind my decision to talk to two wealthy entrepreneurs before concluding my investigation into Angry Young Turkey.

One month into the Gezi uprising, on 26 June 2013, the German weekly magazine *Der Spiegel* published an issue devoted to the events in Turkey. 'Beugt Euch Nicht' ran its cover headline, placed just beneath the image of a European-looking activist holding a sign that inspired *Der Spiegel*'s editors: *Boyun Eğme* it read – don't give in. The chief feature of the magazine was a portrait of Can Öz, a young Turkish entrepreneur who heads one of Turkey's leading publishing houses. The deck of the piece (titled 'Turkish Publisher Can Öz: The Rebellion of an Apolitical Man') presented the young businessman as someone who had followed his father's advice to stay out of politics. 'But the turmoil in Turkey has pushed the leading publisher off the sidelines and into the fray, where he is becoming a key voice of a movement still taking shape.'

As *Der Spiegel*'s Gezi issue hit the shelves in European capitals and in Istanbul (the weekly magazine could still be purchased from newsagents three months after its publication), Öz realized how influential *Der Spiegel* was in defining Europe's perception of Turkey. His company, Can Yayınları (named after him by his late father Erdal Öz, the publisher who made Orhan Pamuk a household name in Turkey) was conducting business talks with the French publishing company Hachette Book Group at the time. Öz wanted to sell some of his company's shares to Hachette, considering this a good move to strengthen his company's financial outlook. The day after *Der Spiegel*'s new issue came out, a Hachette executive e-mailed Öz to ask whether he was indeed the 'leader' of the uprising in Turkey, as this had been the impression she got after reading the article.

Two weeks earlier, on 11 June, Öz had published an article in the British *Guardian* newspaper titled 'I can never trust the Turkish police and government again'. For years he did not speak up enough, he admitted, but no more. 'I could lose everything, but I cannot live a dishonourable life any longer', Öz wrote. It was after he had read this *Guardian* column that the *Der Spiegel* reporter, and Öz's friend Maximilian Popp, decided to profile him. In order to produce a more detailed picture of him, Popp had lived with Öz in his house for a week.

'No, I am not Gezi's leader,' Öz e-mailed back the Hachette executive, 'I am just a businessman doing his best to fulfil his obligations to his country. If we decide to go on with the business arrangement you will get a better idea of the kind of person I am', he joked.

But what kind of a person is this young man who seemed to some readers of *Der Spiegel* as the leader of the Gezi movement? The *Der Spiegel* piece described how 'young, urban middle class is taking to the streets in Istanbul, Ankara and many other Turkish cities. They buy their clothes at Zara, and they fly to London on discount airlines for vacations. They are well-educated and non-ideological.' Why would someone be presented as a leader of such an independent-minded group of people?

When I meet him in a cafe called Cezayir (Algeria in Turkish) this is pretty much how Öz appears: an urban middle-class, well-dressed, cosmopolitan-looking, well-educated young man – and yes, he was once a non-ideological person. When you come to think, it must have been quite difficult for Öz to be unpolitical: his late father Erdal Öz was, after all, one of the most famous chroniclers of the iconic names of Turkish socialism and among the most passionate voices of the left.

Erdal Öz had migrated from Sivas to Istanbul at an early age and became a socialist thanks to a leftist teacher at his high school. Having studied at Ankara University's Law Department in the 1960s, at a time when Turkey's youth was energized by socialist ideas, Öz was imprisoned in the days that followed the military coup of 12 March 1971.

This coup, the second in the history of the republic, came as a shock for Turkey's revolutionaries who were rooting for a different kind of intervention to political power. In the early 1970s, a Turkish political theorist named Doğan Avcıoğlu published a nationalist-socialist newspaper called *Devrim* (Revolution) in which he theorized the so-called 'Millî Demokratik Devrim' (National Democratic Revolution). Widely known as MDD, this revolutionary state was planned to be reached in two steps: first, *ulusalcı* (left-nationalist) military officers would prepare a military coup and take the reins of power, imprison elected politicians associated with the capitalist-bourgeois democratic system and close the parliament. Taking the armed revolution of 1917 in Russia as their model, theoreticians of MDD envisaged the second level as one where young, revolutionary officers of the Turkish army would complete the national revolution by way of giving the reins of power to the proletariat.

Erdal Öz was sympathetic to this view, as were Turkey's numerous leading young intellectuals and journalists. And their dream almost became reality with the first step of the revolution scheduled to be executed on 9 March 1971. There was a problem, however: Turkey's national intelligence agency had intercepted the coup plans and, on 12 March, arrested all the 'revolutionary officers' who were meant to carry them out. The failed coup was then followed by an oppressive climate thanks to which the government could freely lock up leftists. In the aftermath of the 12 March coup, Öz was arrested for his revolutionary activities. Although he was eventually released, his prison time helped the young writer get acquainted with imprisoned young revolutionaries of his country.

In *Gülünün Solduğu Akşam* (The Night When His Rose Withered), first published in 1986, Erdal Öz gave a moving account of the last days of Deniz Gezmiş and Yusuf Aslan, two leaders of Turkey's revolutionary youth movement. They were both executed by hanging aged 25. Öz had incorporated his diary notes and interviews into a nonfiction narrative that told intimate stories of that era's angry young Turks and Kurds.

Öz's wife, meanwhile, came from a bourgeois background. 'She grew up in mansions', Can Öz tells me. 'When my mother's family lost their fortune and influence, she left home, went to Belgium to study archaeology. Upon her return, she started living in Ankara where she met my father.'

According to Öz, his mother's relationship with politics resembled the relationship many Turkish women have with soccer. 'She appeared to support the team her husband supported', he says, laughing.

Having worked for numerous publishers in the past, Erdal Öz set up his own company in 1981, a year after the birth of Can Öz with whose name he christened Can Yayınları. After the foundation of the company, Öz found himself on the wrong side of the law many times; in coup days the books he published were prosecuted, accused of featuring sexually and/or politically degenerate content.

Öz remembers his father's meetings with leftist friends at their apartment. Erdal Öz was both a socialist and an entrepreneur; he wanted to make money from books while doing his best to bring an end to the military dictatorship. 'They were full of hope and anger, despair and rage, love and joy', he says while describing long nights where Erdal Öz and his friends drank *rakı* and discussed the direction of their country.

'Had it not been for my father, there wouldn't be a gram of politics in my life', Öz admits. He clearly remembers the moment his father heard about journalist Uğur Mumcu's assassination. He cried silently inside their apartment as his son watched him in shock. He was aware, also, of the crucial role of Kenan Evren, the leader of the 12 September coup, in his father's life. At their summer house Erdal Öz had named one of the stray cats Kenan, because the cat always stole food from different houses – for Erdal Öz, Kenan was another name, in those years, for thief. 'He loved swearing at that cat,'

Öz remembers, 'it was, for him, a good way of releasing his anger about the president.'

Although he agreed with his father on the harmful character of Evren and militarism, Can Öz quickly realized that things were not quite as black and white as most revolutionaries believed. 'I once believed that the sole victims of military coups were leftists', he tells me. 'Later I learned that this was not the case.' At the time he characterized politicians in the following terms: 'I believed that left-wingers were amateurish; conservatives and nationalists were dangerous; and all politicians were thieves.' Nevertheless, in his life before the Gezi events, Öz's political anger was passive and took the form of complaining and feeling anxious about the future.

He went to Saint Michel, a French lycée in Istanbul where he spent his days kicking footballs, listening to music, reading books and going to the movies. 'Boys were chasing girls and girls were chasing boys', he remembers. 'The rest of our time we spent on finding ways to avoid doing our homework.'

In the days leading to the 28 February 1997 coup, Öz was deeply unsettled by what he saw as the coming tide of Islamism. 'I was afraid of the colour green', he remembers. 'When I saw Islamists on TV, I asked myself whether those guys had what it took to rule Turkey.' Öz describes how his father refrained from pushing him into politics. 'He was not against it but did not show any effort to get me involved either.'

The big difference in Öz's life began after he moved to Boston, Massachusetts to pursue a degree in sociology at Boston University. 'I was interested in computer science and advertising but sociology outweighed all the others.'

I ask him whether he felt freer in Boston. 'Freer? No', Öz replies. 'I was already leading a free life in Turkey before I left.' He smiles and lights a cigarette. 'You see, I was living in

Teşvikiye, as did most of my friends. I used to go to Bodrum for holidays. I was spending all my time in this isolated world. I had little idea about, or interest in, what was going on in the rest of the country.'

Öz describes his undergraduate self as one 'who lived in private schools off his parents' money'. In Boston, he says, the only difference was being so far away from his family. 'Living in a separate house was a luxury. And for the first time in life, I was earning my own money, working night shifts at the university library. I would work from midnight to eight in the morning. They paid me with special rates.'

Some nights, after hours, Öz would watch news footage from Turkey in the dimmed library of Boston University. Images of Recep Tayyip Erdoğan addressing big crowds and winning elections would unsettle him. Öz was anxious about Erdoğan's super-fast rise to the highest echelons of Turkish political power.

Before his second year at Boston University kicked off, Öz visited Istanbul to meet his parents and tell them about his experiences. During a long dinner party, where big amounts of *rakı* were consumed by family members, the conversation took an abrupt turn. Öz was irritated by the way his father spoke down to him. 'I was the typical adolescent', Öz remembers, his brow clouded by the memory of the moment. 'I criticized the way my father talked when he got very angry and I ended up leaving the table and the house.'

Öz's falling out with his father left him in a curious position: a Boston University dropout and the son of a publishing tycoon, he now had to take care of his own life. Starting a new life in the capital Ankara, Öz worked as a waiter, planning to continue with his college education at Ankara's Hacettepe University sometime in the future.

'I was not particularly imagining a career in waitering', Öz jokes. 'I wanted to attend the Women's Studies programme at Hacettepe University and from there hoped to jump to advertising where I could pursue a career.'

But before he could execute this plan, his father located Öz in Ankara and placed a large envelope in his hand. What was in that envelope, he wondered – some money perhaps? It was the manuscript of a book that he wanted his son to translate for Can Yayınları.

Accepting the offer, Öz finished the job assigned to him and came to Istanbul to pay his father a visit. 'Stay here and work with me,' Erdal Öz told him, 'then you can go back to Massachusetts and finish your school there.' This offer was too good to refuse; Öz gave up his plans to become a self-made man and began working at his father's company.

Things were looking brighter than ever. It was a great few weeks when father and son reconciled, getting past their disagreements. They formed a productive partnership: the son pointing out problems in the company and the father enjoying his son showing so much interest in his business. But at the end of that month the cheery mood changed as Erdal Öz told his son that he had terminal lung cancer and not long to live.

By then it was clear that Öz would not be able to get his degree from Boston University. 'Following the death of my father, there was a silent consensus in the family about me taking the reins of the company and becoming its director. This brought to my life a major change: for the first time in life I was taking responsibility for others – not just my family and Can authors but also all the people who worked at the publishing house.'

It was this sense of responsibility that would be the key to Öz's transformation from an unpolitical man to the assumed leader of the Gezi uprising. 'Taking responsibility is the beginning of politicization', Öz muses. 'When you are responsible for others, you feel this huge pressure. I was afraid that I didn't have what it took to run the company. But people around me were really helpful.' Thanks to Öz's managing skills the company increased its sales and attracted the interest of the new hipster generation. Öz's initial strategy had been to preserve the company in its current form to the best of his abilities. 'I was like, "I should not damage this company, it should just continue as it is".'

This plan changed with the Gezi uprising when Öz made the consequential decision to play a major role in the events. 'I wanted to take care of people around me.' This was, in a way, a Sartrean decision – a sudden realization of one's responsibilities to history and the public. 'I was constantly on the lookout for people in need of help. The mood in Gezi was like an avalanche: it grew in time and in force. Young people contributed to each other's courage and energy.' Öz was among those who invited others to the park. When the invitation came from such a well-connected and central figure of the cultural world, people listened. Öz also made the decision to close the publishing house during the events so that all his employees would be able to go to the park. He organized press conferences, published statements supportive of the uprising, and urged all his author and publisher friends to do the same and support the anti-government protests.

'It seems my proactive approach worked in the sense I expected', he says. 'Many authors I work with told me in person how they had one less thing to worry about after seeing my outspoken attitude. I emboldened some people and they did the same thing to others. If I stayed silent during the events I would feel terrible afterwards. I am happy to have fulfilled my share of responsibilities.'

By September 2013, Öz's political stance started transforming not only the cultural world of his country but also the company named after him. He talked to the company staff to inform them about their new direction. Those who seemed to underperform were laid off. During the first week of that month, Öz hired a new editorial director who, in a public statement, emphasized the importance of her new role:

> In June 2013 we witnessed events in our lives the likes of which were never seen in this country ... It changed many things in our lives for good. We saw how creative we can be together and how much fun we can have together and how much power we gain together and how we can use that power to transform things. I am sure that many of us, seeing these developments, decided to make changes in their lives. This is why, starting this September, I will be taking on the role of chief editor at Can Yayınları.

Before we part in the spacious garden of Cezayir restaurant, Öz tells me about his satisfaction with the decisions he made during the uprising, acknowledging how they have thoroughly transformed his business. 'In Turkey's business world, not taking any risks today is to sign one's death warrant and that is what I have refrained from doing', he says, before taking his coat and putting it on. He sounds both businesslike and political – a curious combination of the entrepreneur and the rhetorician. 'I wanted people to see that I was not afraid one bit. I wanted them to see that I would be outspoken from now on and so would my business. In the two years that followed, the silence which I once shared has come to a decisive end. Now, everyone is speaking out.' With Öz's departure, the restaurant becomes silent when I, too, decide to leave.

The Istanbul headquarters of the AK Party is located in Sütlüce, part of Istanbul's Haliç region – known in English as the Golden Horn. It is a warm day in 2015 and I start walking on Haliç's shores, realizing what a curious geographical formation the Golden Horn is. The place is named after its horn-shaped urban waterway that stands at the connecting point of the Sea of Marmara and the Bosphorus Strait. I very rarely come here and I now wonder why I don't walk on these shores more often. Haliç's blue, shiny surface is mesmerizing. It separates the old, ancient part of Istanbul from the rest of the city where I have spent my whole life.

It was from here, from the Golden Horn, that the seeds of New Rome were first sown; Ottomans became a worldwide power only after conquering these shiny waters. The waterway is named 'golden' because, for centuries, ships laden with goods have entered the city from this anfractuous waterbody. During the 1970s and 1980s, the Golden Horn lost its charm when the waterway became infamous for its pollution and horrid odour. It smelled like death; I remember my father searching for alternative routes to use while driving his family in Istanbul so that we would not breathe in the awful smell of the Golden Horn. But the smell was impossible to ignore and it remained that way until the late 1990s and early 2000s when the waterbody was cleaned by the former conservative mayor of Istanbul. Proud of his achievement, he had famously swum through the cold waves of the Golden Horn. As I walk past the AK Party's Istanbul headquarters overlooking the historic waterway, the Golden Horn acquires its magical quality again – the sun shines beautifully on its surface and I get the feeling that the impression of its reflection will stay with me throughout the day.

Less than a hundred metres away from the party headquarters stands the headquarters of MÜSİAD, the Association of Independent Industrialists and Businessmen. There I am set to interview Yavuz Fettahoğlu, the head of MÜSİAD's youth branch, Genç MÜSİAD (Young MÜSİAD). Dressed in an exquisite suit, he is accompanied by a handsome colleague who also manages the organization's digital marketing strategy. They welcome me inside a conference room in the centre of which stands a huge desk covered by LCD screens, keyboards and telephones. This is, Fettahoğlu tells me, where MÜSİAD's call centre used to operate.

Unlike its historic locale, MÜSİAD's history does not stretch far back: it was founded in 1990, 19 years after the foundation of TÜSİAD, the Turkish Industry and Business Association. While the latter organization is seen as the representative and voice of the Istanbul bourgeoisie with strong ties to global capitalism (it had forced the socialist prime minister Bülent Ecevit out of power after issuing a statement in 1979 that criticized his leftist government's lack of encouragement of private entrepreneurship), MÜSİAD has a reputation for being the voice of conservative, pious, 'Anatolian tiger' entrepreneurs based largely in Turkey's Asian cities. The organization is known to parallel the views and methods of the conservative government in the business world.

As the youth leader of this young organization, Fettahoğlu is in an interesting position. He can trace his family ancestry to the Orkhon Inscriptions, the first known records of Turkish existence, erected in the Orkhon valley in Mongolia in the early eighth century. 'I belong to the most ancient and largest of Turkish families', Fettahoğlu tells me. He is not yet 30; the company he represents has been around for 25 years; and yet Fettahoğlu is aware of representing something historical – an ancient, ageless Turkish tradition of conquering economically and doing business in conquered lands.

'The root of our family name "Fettahoğlu" is *fettah* [conqueror] which comes from *fetih* [conquer]', he explains. 'My ancestors were the ones sent to newly conquered Ottoman territories where they spread Turkish culture.' Both the Seljuq dynasty and the Ottoman Empire employed his family, which has its roots in Central Asia. Some members migrated to the Middle East while others settled in the Osmaniye region of Anatolia; there are some Fettahoğlu family members who lived in eastern Anatolia, in cities like Urfa, for decades. 'My ancestors lived mainly around the Black Sea city of Trabzon; in places like Rize.' In Fettahoğlu's estimation, his family has 380,000 members under 138 different surnames. A special foundation dedicated to the family, which has provided him with those numbers, explores the ancestry of Fettahoğlus. 'In Ottoman times, most Fettahoğlu people were farmers', Fettahoğlu tells me. 'This tradition of entrepreneurship continues to this day; we don't have many civil servants among us – most members of the Fettahoğlu family are merchants.'

Born in 1985, he still remembers the bleak atmosphere of his childhood years, which he characterizes as economically painful. 'We were affected by the economic crises that came every five years. I remember my family getting richer, my parents buying new cars and houses and giving me and my little brother new toys and garments for months on end

– then, at the end of the fifth year, we would lose everything because of a major economic crisis.'

Fettahoğlu's father, Asaf Fettahoğlu, had lived in Germany in his youth before deciding to return to his homeland to do commerce. He set up Yenilik Makina (Novelty Machines) in 1986, specializing in the sale of heavy equipment (construction machines and mortar pumps). The company was a pioneer in the construction industry in the late 1980s with its fleet of machines and has been doing very well since the noughties, the decade most strongly associated with Turkey's construction boom.

Fettahoğlu was strongly impressed by stories told in their house. His father told him about the 1970s, an era so violent that he had been unable to go to college. 'He couldn't get a degree because of those who created anarchy on Turkey's streets', Fettahoğlu says. 'In those years my father witnessed the cold face of the Turkish state. I have always admired him for managing to become such a successful entrepreneur in the face of all these problems ... People like my father were seen as members of *halk* [ordinary people] instead of the privileged individuals of this country, referred to as *vatandaş* [citizens]. My father taught me to be proud of being part of ordinary folk.'

Fettahoğlu remembers how elder figures in his family had supported both the liberal ANAP (the Motherland Party) and Necmettin Erbakan, the leader of the Welfare Party. Today's leading conservative politicians speak to a demographic that is arguably a mixture of these two traditions: conservative individuals who are very skilled at doing business while dutifully performing religious rituals required from Muslims, and are represented in the business world by Fettahoğlu's organization.

'My family has a long history of holding pious and conservative values', Fettahoğlu says, recounting how his family had wanted him to attend an Imam Hatip school (*khatip* refers to the person who reads the Islamic sermon), the vocational schools founded to give education to imams employed by the secular government. 'One needed good grades to enrol at an Imam Hatip', he says. 'My grades were good enough to get me a place at the Imam Hatip school in Kartal. But the class I could enter with my grades was part of a German-instructed department, so I had my doubts.'

At the time, all the video games he played, all the films he watched and all the songs he listened to were in English, so it was not surprising that Fettahoğlu preferred English to be the language of instruction in his academic life.

His love for the English language led Fettahoğlu to a private college located in the conservative Şirinevler neighbourhood; he got the highest grade at the entrance exam and was provided with a scholarship during his entire time there. 'It was a boarding school and studying there taught me an awful lot', Fettahoğlu says. 'Living away from my parents was a big advantage that taught me how to stand on my own two feet. I was given the chance to create my own social network and take responsibility for my well-being.'

During the second year of high school, just as Fettahoğlu was getting used to the boarding school environment, Turkey's General Staff issued a military ultimatum, the so-called 28 February coup, announcing that schools like the one Fettahoğlu attended would now be scrutinized by the state apparatus. 'Islamic practices and courses' being taught there, according to the generals, had to be stopped immediately. Imam Hatip schools were also affected by the coup, when it was made more difficult for students to enter colleges because of a deliberate decrease (brought about by a new system of calculation of credits) in their high school grades.

Since he was a big fan of Necmettin Erbakan, the Islamist leader to whom the generals gave the ultimatum, Fettahoğlu's father was outraged by these developments. He was shocked and offended to see the administration of Fettahoğlu's boarding school comply with the demands of the generals.

'Our school administration supported the coup and adopted the new system', he remembers. 'When I first enrolled, this was a boys-only boarding school. After the ultimatum, it started offering mixed-sex education. They removed from the school premises all objects and artefacts associated with Islam. Here was a school that boys like me had attended to have a modern and Islamic education. Now the Islamic aspect of our education was being surgically removed from the curriculum.'

Fettahoğlu's father would have none of it; he took his son out of the school immediately. It was time for the young Fettahoğlu to leave the boarding school and come back home – a major event for the young pupil that he describes today as a 'downfall'.

'At boarding school, fellow pupils were not only my friends, they had become my family – my brothers.' Fettahoğlu is still upset while recounting the day he was forced to leave school. I can see how moved he still is. 'We had this incredible connection between us and I was devastated to see it destroyed because of the 28 February coup.'

In those days Fettahoğlu had struggled to understand his father's decision to take him out of the school. 'He talked to me very openly and earnestly, as if I was a mature person. He described why he had made this decision and I agreed with him. I still do. It was the right thing to do.'

Even today Fettahoğlu has not forgiven those responsible for the coup. 'The coup formed the ways in which I thought about life', he tells me.

After he returned to his parents' home in Kartal, Fettahoğlu found himself in a different world. Many of his childhood friends were going to the Kartal Anadolu Imam Hatip high school; outside the school he witnessed the continual presence of riot police. Cops expected trouble from pupils who were no longer allowed to enter their school premises because of the new regulations drafted by the coup generals.

'In those days, I experienced police violence first hand', Fettahoğlu says. 'At the time, our sisters, all the female pupils who attended these schools, were stopped at the school gates only because of their headscarves. Our brothers rightly objected to this injustice.' From the window of his room and on the street Fettahoğlu would watch the police as they formed a security cordon to stop girls from entering the school. Those outside the gates protesting for them would be attacked. 'They were not just passive guardians of the new regulations – they actively fought against us. My generation has experienced this brutality', Fettahoğlu says, his voice shaking.

Now that he was living with his parents again, Fettahoğlu was more relaxed, but this cost him his sense of discipline, which affected his academic career in the worst way imaginable. Enrolled at a new state school, he started seeing differences between private schools and state schools. In his new school, there were few technical facilities compared to his previous school where he had prepared for maths olympics and had dreams about becoming a software engineer. There he had access to the internet and computer labs where he could put his coding skills to the test; in the new school there was little more than textbooks propagating the state ideology. 'There I lost interest in maths; my grades started dropping. There I learned what state education really means.'

By 2003, this successful student, who had dreams of becoming a software engineer, found himself enrolled in the geophysical engineering department of a state university in Sakarya; it was not among Turkey's top colleges and was certainly not his first choice, but Fettahoğlu decided to make the best of his time there.

Once again, living away from his parents helped Fettahoğlu with his academic career; he won a scholarship in Germany and took a plane to Berlin to study at the Technical University of Berlin. 'I thought about staying in Berlin and not coming back to Turkey. I realized how this was very much the dilemma my father had experienced in his youth', he remembers. 'In the following months I changed my mind, seeing how mechanical German society was. I did not want to become an academic there either. I had this desire to do commerce and I wanted to do it in Turkey. I felt obliged to go back to my country and continue what my father had started. His company had been active for the last 25 years. I wanted to bring it forward.'

Fettahoğlu talks about how the construction sector has massively progressed in Turkey over the last decade. This is something he takes great pleasure from. 'We reached this point where it is clear who the key players in the field are. We are doing business with the world now; we help build cities, we work in neighbouring countries. We sell construction machines and in the world of general contractors we are among the best in the world.'

He is aware that the construction industry is blamed for what has been going on in Turkey during the last decade. The apparent reason why people went to Gezi Park during the uprising in 2013 was to protest against the construction of a shopping mall. When I ask Fettahoğlu about these criticisms, he smiles before coming up with an answer. 'I find those criticisms funny', he says. 'In the past, leftists saw banks as their enemy. Now it is the construction sector that has been made a scapegoat. I totally understand criticisms against inequality in the construction sector; there is certainly big amounts of inequality in the distribution of money. But then again, there is nothing more wrong than accusing the construction sector for all the problems in the country. Construction is a big world that opens doors to numberless little worlds of industry: when you construct a new building you need a lot of components which directly come from industry. When you sell an apartment, people buy stuff to furnish the interior and purchase washing machines that need maintenance. Both sales and service industries prosper.'

I ask him about criticisms concerning the gentrification of cities and how the kind of new buildings his company helps build have been destroying the silhouette of the city. 'I agree wholeheartedly', he says. 'I agree that the new TOKI buildings, those mass housing projects, are ugly. They are meant to provide cheap housing for people desperately in need of housing. We can discuss if those buildings are architecturally beautiful or not. And I also object to unplanned urbanization.' He pauses for a moment. 'But is Istanbul's urbanization really unplanned? I beg to disagree. I live in Kurtköy which has lately seen a considerable amount of construction work. Obviously those constructions are made according to a plan, as they should be. The city administration leaves spaces for green areas and takes the utmost care in building new roads.'

What about destroying the city's heritage with new constructions every day? 'Istanbul is under threat of a massive earthquake so it is important to rebuild ancient houses', he tells me. 'Look at Kadıköy, where many of the buildings are more than a century old. The construction quality of these structures is absolutely terrible. This poses great risk for citizens living there. The streets are narrow – in case of an emergency, rescue teams can't enter them. And those old buildings are so very hard to renovate. They should be rebuilt, that is the only option. Maybe there are some problems with that strategy. But they are far outnumbered by its advantages.'

What about the Emek Theatre, whose planned destruction by a construction firm created so much outrage and was seen as among the reasons behind the uprising? 'Construction companies can and should develop alternative methods for dealing with historical buildings like Emek', Fettahoğlu says. 'It can be technically difficult, even expensive, but such historic buildings should be preserved. The same goes for green areas. They must be preserved as much as possible.'

The conversation leads, inevitably, to the uprising in 2013. 'The government had a clear stance during the events', he says. 'What they said was, "we will move these trees, before pledging to plant new ones".' Fettahoğlu draws a parallel between the debate around Gezi Park and Stuttgart 21, the much discussed urban development project in Stuttgart, Germany. Concerned about the geological and environmental effects of the project, German political parties Alliance '90 and the Greens had organized a massive protest campaign to take the issue to a referendum. 'The city wanted to renovate the railway station and create new railways', Fettahoğlu says.

209

'Protestors wanted respect for the cultural heritage and to save the Schlossgarten Park.' In 2010, he was in the city as more than 50,000 demonstrators clashed with riot police, who used similar tactics to those of their Turkish colleagues.

'For the high-speed rail project the construction company needed to cut centuries-old trees. The government pledged to replant them. Protestors did not believe them. There was chaos on the streets. Police used force in both Stuttgart 21 and Gezi. The difference was in the way those events were reported; the international media couldn't care less about the Stuttgart protests but they used the protests at Gezi for their anti-conservative agendas.' And what would happen if the Turkish government took its plans to a referendum, Fettahoğlu wonders, reminding me how almost 60 per cent of Stuttgart's population voted in favour of the continuation of the project. Apparently, not everyone is against such construction projects. In the municipal elections held on 30 March 2014, six months after the Gezi uprising came to a pause, conservatives won Istanbul, achieving 47.9 per cent of the vote.

At the time of the Gezi uprising, Fettahoğlu was the vice-chairman of Genç MÜSİAD and watched events anxiously. 'We pious people are not huge fans of the police', he tells me, while describing his initial confusion about what stance he should take about the whole thing. 'We have experienced the cold face of police violence in our youths. So, to be frank with you, we did not really know how to interpret the uprising during its first days. We had socialist friends who went there and we didn't say anything against them. I have full respect for those who went there during the first three days. We really couldn't comprehend why the police acted the way they did, burning young people's tents and all.' Another pause. 'But in the days that followed, from the fourth day onwards, events took a different, more violent, turn. It was obvious that this was staged, a well-executed plan, managed partly from outside Turkey. It was after this realization that we decided to make our voice about the uprising heard.'

In July 2013, MÜSİAD leader Nail Olpak gave an interview to Haber 7 news channel about the uprising, voicing his organization's support for people's right to protest. 'But resorting to violence is not acceptable', Olpak warned. 'This was our initial interpretation of the events, on 1 June.' Their philosophy as MÜSİAD was to 'to understand and not "otherize" one another', according to the statement.

Olpak was among the 250 business leaders who visited Tunisia and Algeria as part of Erdoğan's entourage in June 2013. 'Our trip was unprecedented in Turkey's history,' he said in the interview, 'and yet it was left in the background because of the uprising ... We had gone there for the future of this country.' In his analysis of the events, Olpak talked at length about Angry Young Turkey. 'Some young people who attended those events were born during the reign of the AK Party', he said. 'They have little idea about water shortages, mountains of garbage, or 7,200 per cent overnight rates. They know nothing about the past because they have not experienced it.' Finally he talked about his organization's determination to protect law and order: 'We are okay with people's right to free expression but if you insult this country's prime minister, if you harm public property, if you harm private property, if you break the law, then this can only be called protest terror. We are against it and ... will not allow it to happen.'

Fettahoğlu is of the same view. 'We cannot support vandalism and violence on the streets', he says. 'During the events, we continually asked for calm. We asked young people to think about what they had been doing on the streets. We asked them to come and talk to us about what was wrong in their lives. We wanted to learn where this hatred came from. Why were people so full of resentment? We wanted to get an answer.'

With this objective in mind, young MÜSİAD members went to the park to watch the atmosphere first hand. 'According to the analysis of our young friends, protestors didn't really know what they were there for', Fettahoğlu says. 'If young people are getting politicized, they should do so consciously, and become aware of the reasons why they are there. If they adopt an ideology, they should be aware about what the ideology really promises to its followers.'

They then conducted a study among more than 4,500 young people, asking them what the biggest problem in their life was. 'Fourteen per cent had no answer to that question. Just imagine, not a single word. I find this incredible. How can they not have an answer?'

A line of anger forms on Fettahoğlu's brow as he describes a more personal memory from that summer. 'One day in June 2013, we were driving on Bağdat Street with my wife. A friend of ours who was pregnant was sitting in the back seat. Protestors had blocked the street. I couldn't move my car. I have a *tuğrâ* [the calligraphic seal Ottoman sultans had used for signing official documents] in my car. I opened the window and told them to open the road for us. When protestors saw the *tuğrâ* inside the car, they started acting weirdly. They tilted the car. I opened the window again to tell them there was a pregnant lady inside but they didn't listen.

They were like, "you are not getting out of here". I told them this was a big mistake. I was beside myself with anger ... I looked at their faces and I saw the hatred. So I stuck my head outside the window and shouted: "clear the way or I will run you over with my car!"'

Once Fettahoğlu accelerated the car, people started kicking it from four directions. 'Our pregnant friend was no fan of the government. But after this experience, her opinions changed. She understood the danger from people who don't obey them.'

Once he concludes his story, Fettahoğlu seems calmer. 'What I just told you about is not the result of politicization', he says. 'It is the result of a sort of void. People are radicalized and they act like hooligans. Politicization should be an intellectual process ... To hate the other side', Fettahoğlu says, 'is not, cannot be, politicization. No.' A final pause. 'It is only hatred in ignorance.'

There is a Judas tree in Haliç Park just outside the MÜSİAD headquarters. Its pink flowers look beautiful under the sun. I stand under this Judas tree while looking at Eyüp, the Istanbul district on the other side of the shore. I am reminded of this place's historic significance as I watch the flowing waters of the Golden Horn. I have begun my journey a few metres away from Gezi Park and, after many months, finally arrived at Haliç Park, which is, at the moment, deserted but for me.

Will the financial prowess of conservatives continue to spread from this horn-shaped urban waterway to the rest of the country, all the way to the Bosphorus Strait and the Sea of Marmara? Will the old, ancient world of Ottomans and their modern-day political representatives, the conservatives, continue to build their New Turkey from this place where the seeds of New Rome had first been sown? Will the golden waterway of Haliç preserve its charm and attract goods-laden ships from neighbouring countries to Turkey?

Standing in the shade of the Judas tree and looking at the sun's beautiful reflections on Haliç's surface, I think about all the young people I have been talking to during the previous year. Many of them had struggled against the ideology represented in the buildings standing just behind me: the headquarters of MÜSİAD and the governing party, the latter protected by machine-gun-carrying riot cops.

Looking at the large, white clouds above, I remember all the anger that I have been witnessing in the young people whom I have interviewed. The contrast between their passion and the calm of the Golden Horn couldn't be more striking. Two cops passing by the park eye me somewhat suspiciously as I decide to head back home.

# EPILOGUE

# The Night of the Coup

I had just finished reading the first proofs of this book when, on 15 July 2016, a group of soldiers in the Turkish army executed a plan to topple the Turkish government. At around 10 p.m. local time, soldiers occupied Istanbul's Fatih Sultan Mehmet and Boğaziçi bridges, their tanks firing at those who came there to protest. Army helicopters attacked the police headquarters in Ankara, machine guns firing bullets from the air in scenes reminiscent of a Hollywood film. High-ranking officers shot at ordinary people at random and occupied the headquarters of CNN Türk and the public broadcaster TRT, throwing journalists out of the control rooms at gunpoint. A small group went to the headquarters of the *Daily Sabah* newspaper and fired shots at the newsroom. In between Gezi Park and the Republic Monument at Taksim Square, soldiers fired at those out for a walk, ordering them to clear the squares immediately. 'There has been a coup,' one of them shouted. 'Go home.'

Was this what the long-awaited 'Turkish uprising' looked like? The US state department's consular service tweeted shortly after midnight: 'The Turkish government states elements of Turkish army attempting uprising'. At the same time, a 40-strong squad team of maroon berets arrived at a hotel in Marmaris where President Erdoğan was on holiday. Specially trained soldiers made their way into his room, killed his aides, put hundreds of bullets into the furniture and prepared to execute the president. But Erdoğan was nowhere to be found.

He emerged on television sometime later, speaking via FaceTime, asking his followers to fill the squares and stand strong against the uprising. While security forces attempted to contain the coup plotters, many buildings were under blockade. At around three in the morning, helicopters started bombing the Turkish parliament. The national intelligence building was bombed, as were thousands on the streets who came out in defence of the status quo. F16 jets aerially refuelled from Turkey's Incirlik airbase (normally used to bomb Islamic State targets by the coalition) approached key buildings in Ankara and Istanbul, flying low and producing sonic booms that crushed the windows of houses. People were thrown on the floor, saying their farewells to loved ones, mistaking the jet sounds for bombs. On the streets of Ankara, tanks ran over cars and protestors, forcing people to jump from bridges. There were gory images of the bodies of ordinary people cut into two. Elderly women and teenagers were among those shot during the events. More than 200 died and 1,500 were wounded.

In Cihangir, the heart of the Gezi uprising, there was no sign of any appetite for a military coup. In the nearby Tophane neighbourhood, people rushed to the streets and drove their cars to Atatürk Airport, which had been seized by soldiers during the night. The parliament was bombed again and the prime minister ordered the shooting down of jets flown by coup plotters, placing the blame for the uprising on the exiled cleric Fetullah Gülen and his followers in the military. More than eighty thousand state employees suspected of having ties with the movement would be suspended or dismissed from work in the aftermath of the failed coup.

In a strange symmetry with the events in 2013 which are the focus of some of this book, people filled Gezi Park and Taksim Square in the following days. For the past three years the square had been closed to any public demonstration, a symbol of Turkey's strange relationship with repression, but now, following the attempted coup, people were asked to fill it. Powerful politicians started talking about the value of free media and the flow of information. Public transport was declared free of charge. There was little police presence in Gezi and the atmosphere resembled Hyde Park. Public figures were making speeches and people seemed ecstatic to be on the streets.

As I headed to my apartment in Cihangir at about 3 a.m., four days after the coup, I found myself among young Turks and Kurds who had rushed to Taksim from the most distant corners of Istanbul. I saw Syrian refugees. There were body-builders riding on motorbikes. A group of young men had filled the back of an old truck and were singing songs. I saw headscarved women and girls in mini-skirts, walking in the same direction. Overwhelmed with the events in this young and always youthful republic, I started crying.

# Further Reading

## Books

*A Strangeness in My Mind*, Orhan Pamuk (Faber & Faber)
Mevlut, the protagonist of Turkish Nobelist Orhan Pamuk's 2014 novel, is a young Anatolian boy who arrives in Istanbul in 1969. In the decades that follow he witnesses violent clashes between Turkey's radical left and ultra-right militants. Although his heart is with the progressives, the romantic Mevlut detests the violence from both sides and Pamuk shows how it made life horrid and unliveable for working-class people like his protagonist. This is essential reading for anyone willing to understand the rationale of Turkish *homo-economicus*, the ordinary Turks who have no wealthy family to fall back on.

*Muslim Nationalism and the New Turks*, Jenny White (Princeton University Press)
As a distinguished cultural anthropologist, White has conducted a unique field study on the rise of 'the new Turks' (pious Turks who combine capitalism and religion in their lives) which is second to none for its meticulousness and insights. From right-wing nationalists to Kemalists to conservatives, White's scope is refreshingly broad. Her lengthy interviews with her subjects slowly reveal the underlying tensions of a fantastically politicized society.

*The Genesis of Young Ottoman Thought: A Study in the Modernization of Turkish Political Ideas*, Şerif Mardin (Syracuse University Press)
This is the best study, in any language, of the intellectual worlds of Young Ottomans. Turkey's leading social scientist Mardin reads through Ottoman archives, showing how the rise of the print media accompanied the rise of public intellectuals (Sadık Rıfat Paşa, Şinasi, Mustafa Fazıl Paşa, Namık Kemal, Ziya Paşa, Ali Suavi and Hayreddin Paşa) during the nineteenth century. The publishing activities of those Young Ottomans ran hand-in-hand with their flourishing political careers. The book provides a nice opportunity to reflect on parallels between the rise of social media in 2010s Turkey and the printing presses in the mid-nineteenth century and ask whether what Mardin calls a new 'climate' of opinion has contributed to the political upheaval in the country.

*The Young Turks and the Boycott Movement: Nationalism, Protest and the Working Classes in the Formation of Modern Turkey*, Doğan Çetinkaya (I.B.Tauris)
This is an eye-opening book on the political foundations of the Young Turks and their boycott movement. A strong and curious combination of nationalist and socialist discourses, the Young Turks' politics would define Turkey for the rest of the twentieth century. Their plan to construct a new political system from the people up proved popular; there are undeniable links between their dreams and those of Gezi protestors and also a curious mixture of socialists and Turkish nationalists.

*The Time Regulation Institute*, Ahmet Hamdi Tanpınar (Penguin Classics)

The uneasy co-existence of modernity and tradition, and the forces of order and freedom in Turkey's political life have yet to find a better fictional expression. The protagonist of Tanpınar's 1961 novel, Hayri İrdal, spends his youth in the streets of Istanbul, and takes part in the foundation of an ambitious project to set all Turkish clocks to proper, central time. This brilliant allegory of Turkish centralization features echoes of ideas of Young Ottomans and Young Turks, and their conflicting projects of protecting traditions and wanting to upset them.

*Turkish Awakening: A Personal Discovery of Modern Turkey*, Alev Scott (Faber & Faber)

Alev Scott was an assistant director in opera before she came to live in Istanbul and this shows in her passionate, colourful depiction of Turkey. Daughter of a British father and a Turkish mother, Scott meets numerous Turkish youngsters in Istanbul's universities, offices and public squares and is endlessly fascinated by their desires and dreams.

## Magazine articles

'Ottomania', Elif Batuman, *New Yorker*, February 2014

This moving, personal account of the changes in Turkey's cultural sphere, as rendered by the Turkish American Batuman, provides a fascinating perspective on the rise of nostalgia for the Ottoman past in modern-day Turkey. Ottomania has fuelled creative industries even while it gave rise to intense political conflict.

'Occupy Gezi: From the Fringes to the Center and Back Again', Alexander Christie-Miller, *White Review*, July 2013 (http://www.thewhitereview.org/features/occupy-gezi-from-the-fringes-to-the-centre-and-back-again/)
Since moving to Istanbul in 2010, Alex Christie-Miller of the London *Times* had been observing the country's political tribulations, documenting the legal flaws and inconsistencies of the so-called 'coup plots' that rocked Turkish politics in the latter half of the noughties. A visit to an Antony and the Johnsons concert in Istanbul, observations of Turkish and Kurdish youths during the Gezi protests and moving depictions of the city help make Christie-Miller's piece among the best accounts of the events of summer 2013.

'Letter from Balat', Nagihan Haliloğlu, Full Stop, April 2016 (http://www.full-stop.net/2016/04/06/blog/nagihan-haliloglu/letter-from-balat/)
In this beautifully observed piece, a literature professor visits Balat, an Istanbul neighbourhood that has experienced heavy doses of gentrification during the 2010s. She writes about how Balat has 'changed from a neighborhood of mostly working-class, religious families into a haunt for hip and secular culture vultures.' Inside a coffee house Haliloğlu plays a game, trying to figure whether customers are observant Muslims or hipsters and discovering how difficult a task that is: "The mollas, some of whom have trickled down from the hill with their baggy trousers and cloaks, are easy to spot, but then there are the observant Muslim middle classes who are more difficult to tell apart from the hipsters."

## Websites

Bianet English (http://bianet.org/english)
Funded by the European Commission, the Independent Communication Network (BIA in Turkish) was founded in 2000. Specializing in coverage of human rights and democracy issues in Turkey, the agency's English website features lengthy analyses of youth, violence and women.

Agos (http://www.agos.com.tr/en/home)
The English edition of the bilingual (Armenian and Turkish) weekly newspaper once edited by the slain journalist Hrant Dink is famous for its coverage of culture and politics.

Daily Sabah (www.dailysabah.com)
The website of the conservative English-language Turkish newspaper provides around the clock coverage of Turkish news and features articles on culture and politics written from a conservative perspective.

# Index

DEC 0 6 2016